Leslie Vernick's
The Emotionally Destructive Relationship—
a book that meets a need

"Discover what's wrong...find a biblical understanding of God's solution. As you apply what you read, you will learn how to let go of destructive ways and will heal and grow to become healthier and changed by God's loving grace."

—Dr. Catherine Hart Weber,
coauthor of *Secrets of Eve* and *Unveiling Depression in Women;* Fuller Theological Seminary adjunct professor

"Readers will walk away with a plan of action on how to change themselves and how to change the patterns of their relationships...[Fills] a significant need in the world of Christian counseling."

—Jeffrey Black, PhD,
psychologist; Chair and Professor of the Masters in Christian Counseling at Philadelphia Biblical University

"I could relate to so many of the people mentioned in this book, and it really scared me...I knew I had to make changes in my life and marriage...Leslie uses Scripture to validate the points the makes, which is different than any of the other books I have read...I would highly recommend this book to anyone who is in or has been in an emotionally destructive relationship. It has changed my outlook on my self and my marriage; I am beginning to feel like myself again."

—Jess, a reader

"Connects emotional abuse to its spiritual roots and provides practical tools to help victims heal...Challenges readers to take a united stand against emotional abuse."

—Brenda Branson and Paula Silva,
FOCUS Ministries, Inc.; authors of *Violence Among Us: Ministry to Families in Crisis*

"Provides a critical first step down the path of healing and growth for those who find themselves stuck in abusive relationships...As always, Leslie meets the sufferer and the sinner with compassion, truth, concrete direction, and lots of hope."

—**Winston Smith, MDiv,**
director of Counseling Services and faculty member
at Christian Counseling and Educational Foundation

"This book is a must-read—not only will it educate the reader to take the necessary steps to freedom, but it will also prevent future destructive relationships."

—**Michelle Borquez**
author of *God Crazy: An Adventurous Road Trip to Joyful Surrender;* Host of I-Life television's *Shine*

"Emotional abuse is often overlooked, but...Leslie wonderfully and practically addresses this tough topic that cripples the Body of Christ and our witness to the world."

—**Karl Benzio, MD,**
psychiatrist; founder and Executive
Director of Lighthouse Network

"Here is a book I deeply wish didn't need to be written, but also one I am so grateful Leslie Vernick has had the courage to write. You will be moved by her compassion, be appreciative of her candor, and be helped by her professional skills honed in the trenches of real life."

—**Gene Appel,**
Lead Pastor, Willow Creek Community Church,
South Barrington, Illinois

The Emotionally Destructive Relationship

Leslie Vernick

HARVEST HOUSE PUBLISHERS

EUGENE, OREGON

Cover by Dugan Design Group, Bloomington, Minnesota

Cover photo © Susie Cushner / Graphistock Photography / Veer

ADVISORY

Readers are advised to consult with their physician or other professional practitioner before implementing any suggestions that follow. This book is not intended to take the place of sound professional advice, medical or otherwise. Neither the author nor the publisher assumes any liability for possible adverse consequences as a result of the information contained herein.

THE EMOTIONALLY DESTRUCTIVE RELATIONSHIP
Copyright © 2007 by Leslie Vernick
Published by Harvest House Publishers
Eugene, Oregon 97402
www.harvesthousepublishers.com

Library of Congress Cataloging-in-Publication Data
    Vernick, Leslie.
    The emotionally destructive relationship / Leslie Vernick.
        p. cm.
    Includes bibliographical references.
    ISBN-13: 978-0-7369-1897-8 (pbk.)
    ISBN-10: 0-7369-1897-3
    1. Interpersonal relations—Religious aspects—Christianity. 2. Emotions—Religious aspects—Christianity. I. Title.
    BV4597.52.V47 2007
    248.8'6—dc22
                                                                        2007014155

To men and women I have met—

Those who have trusted God to change them,
have moved beyond being victim or victimizer,
and are becoming who God intended them to be.

ACKNOWLEDGMENTS

My name is on the cover, but many people held up my arms while I was writing this book. Thank you, my faithful prayer team. Without your love and prayers, I'd still be sitting in my chair, staring at a blank page.

Howard, you have been my strongest supporter through each of my books. I am deeply grateful for your encouragement, which helped fan into flames the gifts God has given me. I know your sacrifice, and I love you more for it. Ryan and Amanda, although you're no longer living at home, your encouragement and love have blessed me beyond measure. Theresa Cain, my soul sister and friend, thanks for your continual support and prayers.

Glenna Dameron, Georgia Shaffer, Winston Smith, Jim Cheshire, and Erin Stephens, thank you for reading through my first draft and giving me your valuable feedback. Gary Thomas and Howard Lawler, I appreciate your willingness to dialogue with me about the sticky subject of headship and submission. Marg Hinds, my administrative assistant, thank you for your prayers and everything else you do to keep my office in order.

I am extremely indebted to those individuals and couples who have not only allowed me to bear witness to their brokenness and pain, but to walk with them through their suffering and to be a part of their healing. Thank you from the bottom of my heart. You have taught me so much about patience, grace, truth, and love. When I tell a story, please know that identifying details have been altered so that your confidentiality is protected. In some cases I have blended together people's stories because they were so similar. I hope you feel encouraged that the pain you've experienced might be used in some way to help others.

To the team at Harvest House Publishers, thank you for believing in me and in this book. I appreciate your patience and your kindness in extending my deadlines due to my flooded office. To my editor, Erin Healy, I have loved working with you again. Your keen insights and editorial comments made this a much better book.

And, Lord Jesus, your love seems too good to be true. Thank you for loving me and showing me more and more of your ways. It is an awesome privilege to know you, love you, and serve you. Every day you amaze me!

CONTENTS

~

Part Three: Surviving It

Making a Good Start

When I began to write this book, I decided to start with a nine-day sabbatical, from Friday to the following Monday. I cleared my slate: no clients, no chores, no responsibilities. Nothing but the book. I was anxious to concentrate on pulling together the months of research and reading, thinking and praying that I had done.

Thursday night, I had one more client to see. As I stepped out of my home office into the waiting room, the look on Connie's face told me something was very wrong. She gestured down the hall.

"Um, I think you have a leak or something," she said.

I turned and saw a large pool of brown water creeping toward us. My initial thought was that the washing machine from upstairs was overflowing, but unfortunately the problem was not so benign. As it turned out, my septic system pipe was clogged and had begun spilling foul liquid waste into my office, waiting room, and surrounding storage rooms.

Initially I stayed calm. After all, I wouldn't want one of my clients to think I *couldn't cope with stress!* But my nine-day book-writing sabbatical turned into a stinky, toxic, overwhelming mess. This was no simple cleanup! After the calm gave way to frustration, I mostly just wanted to move out.

Instead I took the first step and called a plumber to unclog the blockage. Next, I received the bad news that all the carpeting in the entire downstairs would have to be ripped out. I am still at this stage as I write. All desks, books and bookcases, computers, couches, suitcases, file cabinets, and boxes and boxes and boxes of storage had to be moved. After that was done, the cement floor had to be scrubbed and detoxified. The contaminated items that had been on the floor had to be thrown out or sanitized. After the new carpet is put in, I somehow have to figure out how to put it all back together, like a 5000-piece jigsaw puzzle.

But as I reflected upon this change of plans, I realized that everything is as it should be. For as I write about toxic relationships and the damage they cause, I will experience firsthand just a bit of the stress of living in a toxic environment, even if it is only for a short time. And as much as I wish it would all go away, it won't. There is no quick or easy solution, and the mess has turned my entire life upside down. From this vantage point, I don't know when life will ever feel normal again.

⁓

Many people feel so overwhelmed by the mess of their painful relationships that instead of taking the appropriate action, they allow the toxicity to spill all over them and their children. They feel helpless and powerless and don't know what to do. Even if they make some initial efforts, the difficulty makes it easier to give up and close their eyes to the obvious destruction all around them.

Please, don't do that. I understand that right now, surviving your destructive relationship feels impossible. I know it's painful and scary to think about what it will take to clean up the mess. But you cannot change something that you will not face.

I can't promise that if you read this book, the destructive person in your life will change.

But I can promise you that if you apply what you read, you will grow and heal and become a healthier individual, which is a good start toward building more loving and healthy relationships.

Introduction

Created to Live Connected

*destroy: 1. to reduce (a thing;) to useless fragments
or a useless form, as by smashing or burning,
injure beyond repair; demolish. 2. to put an end to;
extinguish. 3. to kill; slay. 4. to render ineffective
or useless; neutralize; invalidate.
5. to defeat completely. 6. to engage in destruction.*

*destructive: 1. tending to destroy;
causing much damage... 2. tending to
overthrow, disprove, or discredit; negative.*

For more than 15 years, I didn't see or speak to my mom. Before that time, my contact with her was sporadic and always tense. She didn't attend my wedding, nor was she present when my son was born or my daughter was adopted from Korea. She never shared Christmas with us or invited my family to visit her.

When I was eight years old, my parents went through an ugly divorce. My younger sister, brother, and I went to live with our mother. After we endured Mom's alcoholism and abusive behavior for years, my father finally gained custody of us. My mother remarried and eventually moved to another state. She chose not to stay closely involved with her children.

As a Christian counselor, I have worked with many people stuck in destructive relationship patterns, but I also know what it feels like to be in one. My own painful relationship with my mother began in my childhood, but it did not stop when I grew up. Even as an adult, I feared her temper, we could not communicate, and she would not or could not acknowledge that she hurt me. The helplessness, confusion, frustration, and hurt of such a relationship can be overwhelming. If you've picked up this book, you probably know exactly what I mean. Navigating the pain in a God-honoring way is tricky and sometimes risky.

The title of this book does not begin to describe the damage that occurs in this kind of relationship. A destructive relationship injures more than our emotions. It attacks every part of our lives. It can destroy our very souls.

The Opposite of God's Plan for Us

I wish there weren't a need to write a book on this topic, especially for Christians. Sadly, this material is probably long overdue. When you think of destructive relationships, what comes to your mind first? Most people typically think of relationships that include some kind of physical, verbal, or sexual abuse. Without question, all abusive behavior, whether physical, sexual, or emotional, is always destructive to the personhood of the victim and lethal to the relationship. However, plenty of other sinful relational patterns not necessarily labeled or recognized as abusive are equally harmful.

Picture a lovely white-sided house with a large porch. A bomb can level that house in an instant, but termites or mold take much longer to make their damage known, and their devastating effects may go unnoticed for years. Just as there are numerous ways to destroy a house, a person and a relationship can be wounded or destroyed in lots of different ways. Someone can be undermined, crushed, stifled, and suppressed as well as shattered, demolished, or broken. A relationship is damaged when it's weakened, fractured, or killed through the attitudes and actions of one or both people in the relationship.

You might have sensed for some time now that something inside of you is dying, even if you can't name it or explain why. You might have difficulty talking about it. Maybe people can't see the signs of the damage you feel and don't understand what you're trying to say. Maybe they tell you you're making a mountain out of a molehill, even though you know without a doubt that something has gone wrong, and you fear nothing can be done to reverse the effects.

Relationships that lead to this kind of heartache are the opposite of God's plan for us. Healthy relationships are at the heart of the biblical message because God created us to live connected to one another. The Word focuses on our relationship with God and is full of commands and instructions on how we are to care for and love others as well as ourselves properly. Every one of the Ten Commandments speaks about some aspect of community and what it takes to maintain good fellowship with God and with each other. No one functions well all alone. In the movie *Cast Away*, Tom Hanks powerfully portrayed human intolerance for isolation. Marooned on a desert island, he began having conversations with a volleyball he named Wilson. God specifically designed the human family as well as the church family to provide the close connections our hearts long to experience.

Jesus tells us that there is nothing more important than to learn how to love God and others well (Matthew 22:36-39). Because people are so important to God, he warns us about the painful consequences of destructive relationship patterns. For example, the book of Proverbs says, "With their words, the godless destroy their friends," and, "Telling lies about others is as harmful as hitting them with an ax, wounding them with a sword, or shooting them with a sharp arrow" (Proverbs 11:9; 25:18). Jesus takes the matter of verbal abuse quite seriously when he likens it to murder (Matthew 5:21-22). Many people suffer in relationships where offensive words and threatening gestures are the weapons of choice, used to manipulate, control, punish, and wound without leaving any physical evidence.

The church is finally beginning to acknowledge the reality of physical abuse in Christian homes, but it remains rather silent on the devastating consequences of other forms of abuse and destruction, especially when the damage is not apparent. Physical injuries we see. Bruises, a broken arm, or a black eye is obvious evidence of something dreadfully wrong, and Christians have begun to speak out. Although injuries to someone's soul and spirit are less easily detected, they are just as real and painful as physical injuries, and just as worthy of our attention.

We Christians do not always know how to recognize destructive relationships or validate the deep emotional pain they inflict, nor do we necessarily know how to fix things. My prayer is that this book will help you to see more clearly what's wrong in relationships that hurt you, to identify the underlying heart issues at work in these relationships, and to help you learn how to respond to your specific relationship situations in a biblical, life-giving way.

Finding a Biblical Understanding

Throughout this book, I explain what's happening and what to do about it from a biblical rather than psychological perspective. I do this purposefully. When advocating for people wounded or trapped in destructive relationships, at times I have experienced resistance by Christians and church leaders. They are suspicious (perhaps rightly so) of anything sounding too secular or psychological and therefore find it difficult to hear. If you are in a destructive relationship, I want you to have a biblical understanding and vocabulary of what's happening, so you can figure out what's wrong and what God's solution is.

Making Distinctions

I have divided *The Emotionally Destructive Relationship* into three parts. The first part, "Seeing It," will help you learn *how to distinguish between healthy and destructive relationships*. A self-administered questionnaire at the end of chapter 1 will pinpoint the unhealthy aspects of your relationships so you can see more clearly what's wrong. In chapter 2 I examine the emotional, physical, mental, relational, and spiritual effects of destructive relationships and demonstrate how these patterns are passed down in families. In chapters 3, 4, and 5, I use a biblical model to explain how relationships become unhealthy and describe seven heart attitudes that, if left unchecked, always lead to destructive interactions with people.

Thinking About Your Own Role

In part 2, "Stopping It," I teach you *how to think more biblically about your own role in your relationships* and give you specific strategies to begin to make changes. I want you to know that you don't have to continue living in pain. In chapters 6 and 7 I help you learn how to gather up your courage and resources in order to initiate some crucial dialogue with the other person in the destructive situation. Once you've started that process, chapters 8 and 9 show you when to confront, how to speak the truth in love, and when to step back from the relationship. I give you biblical reasons to support your decisions. If you counsel others, these chapters will provide you with specific steps to help them wisely apply God's truth to their particular situation.

Finding Healing

In part 3, "Surviving It," I *move beyond the relationship to your own healing.* Sadly, many times a destructive relationship does not improve. Sometimes the person you're in relationship with will be unwilling to change or look at themselves in a new way. That does not mean that there is no hope for you. God sees what you're going through and wants to help you heal even if your relationship never does.

One of the first stories in the Bible is about a destructive relationship between two women. Sarai and her husband Abram (their names were later changed to Sarah and Abraham) were unable to conceive any children even though God had promised Abram that he would have many descendants. In those days, it was customary for barren women to give their husbands a surrogate, and so Sarai chose Hagar, her Egyptian handmaiden, to bear a child for them.

When Hagar became pregnant with Abram's child, things deteriorated between her and Sarai. When we're in the habit of relating with others by comparing ourselves to them, we will always see ourselves as either superior or inferior, better or worse. I wonder if Hagar felt inferior to Sarai as the servant. Perhaps Sarai acted superior toward Hagar, as the wife. Regardless, after Hagar became pregnant with Abram's child, the tables turned. "When Hagar knew she was pregnant, she began to treat her mistress, Sarai, with contempt" (Genesis 16:4).

Sarai's response to Hagar's disrespect was understandable but destructive. Sarai avoided taking responsibility for her own feelings and actions by accusing Abram for all this turmoil. Abram refused to get in the middle and told Sarai to handle it herself. She did, by treating Hagar "so harshly that she finally ran away" (16:6). Sarai was envious of Hagar's pregnancy, but she justified her cruelty because of Hagar's contempt.

While Hagar was all alone in the wilderness, pregnant and scared, an angel of the Lord found her, reassured her, and told her what to do. God had heard her cry for help. From then on she used a new name to describe her God, El Roi, meaning *the God who sees*. Sarai and Hagar's relationship problems were far from over, but Hagar found comfort and strength in the truth that God saw her and knew her plight.

In the last part of this book I want you to know, *really know*, that God sees you and deeply loves you. When we have been beaten down by the words or actions of another, we feel broken and helpless, unlovely and unlovable. How wonderful that our healing does not depend upon the love or affirmation or apology of another person. We may never get any of those things. But our strength and healing will come as we are able to receive and believe God's love.

When I finally believed (first with my head and then with my heart) that God loved me, I began healing from the hurt of my mother's rejection. This healing process didn't happen overnight or even in one year, but over time I began to forgive her—not because she asked me to, but because I could. I no longer needed to feel angry or even hurt. I was set free. Free from the past, free from the pain, free to be me. Free to love her. That's what God was doing in me in that 15-year interval. Even then, I never dreamed, hoped, or even prayed that my mother and I would reconcile our relationship. Then one day several years back, everything turned upside down.

My younger sister, Patt, phoned me early one morning. Our mom had just called her complaining of shortness of breath. Because of the way Mom sounded, Patt had told her to hang up and immediately call an ambulance. Now my sister was asking if I would go with her to visit our mother.

God has a way of creating circumstances that expose whether what we say we believe actually translates into authentic faith and trust. Here was my test. Did I really believe him when he told me that I was loved and that he would go into this encounter before me and with me? Did I trust that he would protect me and sustain me? These times of testing are opportunities for us to know God better so that we can grow in genuine faith. That morning I said yes to my sister. More importantly, I said yes to God, not knowing whether my mother would receive me or not.

By faith, I packed my suitcase and got on—and got off—the airplane. With each step forward, I reminded myself again and again of Psalm 27:1—"The Lord is my light and my salvation—so why should I be afraid?" Although my heart felt stronger, my body felt weak as my stomach flip-flopped and my heart pounded. As I walked into Mom's hospital room in intensive care, my knees were knocking, but I was sure of one thing: God was with me and would give me everything that I needed to interact with my mother in a way that honored him. I didn't know what was going to happen or if we would be able to build a new relationship, but I felt something within me that was stronger than my fear of my mother. It was God's love coursing through me, enabling me to think about ministering to her needs without looking for, hoping for, or expecting anything in return. In a wonderful, gradual miracle, Mom and I were able to build a positive and loving relationship, and I had the privilege to care for her in her final weeks of her life and take her to the foot of the cross.

The final chapters in part 3 will show you how you can heal and rebuild your identity according to who God says you are. In the process you will learn to become more and more the person God has created you to be. Like a plant that has been crushed and wilted because of a lack of nourishment and light, as you receive God's love and truth you will burst forth with new blooms. You will start to rewrite your story, not as a victim, but as the victor who is gaining the victory.

My prayers are with you as you begin this process. God will help you. He is your El Roi, the God who sees—sees *you*.

Part One

Seeing It

What Is an Emotionally Destructive Relationship?

*The range of what we think and do
is limited by what we fail to notice.
And because we fail to notice
that we fail to notice
there is little we can do
to change
until we notice
how failing to notice
shapes our thoughts and deeds.*

DANIEL GOLEMAN

One day, unable to contain her pain any longer, Terri blurted to her husband, John, "I would rather die than continue to be married to you." Stunned, John could not fathom why Terri felt this way. He believed they had a good marriage. They were both Christians, loved God, and loved each other, or so he thought.

Yet what felt like a good marriage to John felt like death to Terri. For years she tried to be a good wife, meeting John's needs, loving him as she thought a Christian wife was supposed to love her husband. John loved Terri loving him, and she did it well. John was completely unaware, however, that Terri felt unloved by him.

Throughout their marriage, John was confident, Terri was less sure of herself. Believing that his way was the best way to do things, John embarked upon a mission of helping Terri do things the way he thought she should. At times, John was harsh and gave Terri the impression that her own methods, thoughts, feelings, ideas, and desires were not as wise or as helpful or as spiritual as his.

Sometimes Terri spoke out, but over the years, she found it easier just to keep quiet and go along. She often received affirmation from other Christian women for her quiet and gentle spirit. Eventually, John's overbearing manner undermined Terri's fragile self-esteem and her ability to stand up for her own thoughts and feelings. She began to believe that if she thought or felt differently than John, she was wrong. Over the years, little by little, the person God created Terri to be disappeared.

John's habitual way of relating to Terri was not intentionally malicious; nevertheless, the damage was real. After Terri's blurting incident, they both realized that they each needed to make significant changes (the biblical word is *repent*) in the way they interacted and thought about each other. Only then could they breathe any health back into their marriage and into Terri's fractured sense of self.

Repentance for Terri would involve developing courage so that she could stand up and confront John's overbearing behavior. She would also need to work hard to rediscover and name her own thoughts, feelings, and ideas rather than always deferring to her husband's. Repentance for John would involve learning how to love his wife biblically, which included valuing and encouraging the person God created her to be instead of always trying to change her. He would need to learn humility and change his deeply held belief that his ways were always superior to Terri's.

In another situation, Tom was the associate pastor of a small congregation for several years and loved his ministry. Without warning, his senior pastor asked him to resign. Tom and his family were devastated. They never saw this coming. Certainly Tom and his senior pastor approached ministry differently at times, but Tom believed they worked out their conflicts effectively—at least until the senior pastor told Tom that he was never a good fit in the church. When Tom protested and asked to have a meeting with the elders to discuss this, the senior pastor told Tom he was being divisive, and his unsubmissive attitude was a hindrance to the growth and health of the church. He asked Tom and his family to leave immediately.

Tom struggled. Should he stay and defend himself? Was that God's way of handling this? Why hadn't the senior pastor expressed his concerns before? Why was he asking Tom to leave when it seemed the ministry was flourishing?

Tom was caught by surprise because he believed his relationship with his boss was one way, when in reality it was another. Tom didn't know why the senior pastor wasn't honest with him (or perhaps even with himself), from the start. In the past, he told Tom he was doing a good job and Tom never suspected that his boss didn't mean it.

Tom started to question his boss about his previous performance evaluations. Instead of taking a moment to listen to Tom's concerns and examine his own motives, the senior pastor told Tom that his protests and questions were evidence of his ungodliness. Tom knew then that there was no way they could have an honest discussion about what happened. Their relationship collapsed, their joint ministry was negatively affected, and Tom and his wife left the church crushed.

"We were completely blindsided," Tom sobbed in my office. "I don't know if I can ever trust someone in ministry again. The worst part is that we can't even talk with people about it without making the pastor look bad and hurting the overall ministry of the church. I don't want to do that." He paused.

"Leslie, I loved my job and I loved this man. He was like a father to me. How does someone recover from this kind of betrayal?"

"Not quickly or easily," I said to Tom and his wife. "You will need to allow yourself enough time to be angry, to grieve, to question God, and to heal and grow from this experience."

I also told them, "When someone deeply betrays us and will not take responsibility for the deception, the relationship itself may be beyond repair, at least until the Lord shows this other person his own sin. But you can learn from this situation and move ahead into new relationships with more wisdom. One of the things that might be most helpful eventually is to learn to discern some of the sinful heart themes that are typical in destructive relationships." (I'll address these in chapters 3, 4, and 5.) "Becoming more aware and alert can help you in future relationships so that you are not caught by surprise."

Rita, a fortysomething single woman, lived at home with her mother and father until recently. Rita's parents make most of her decisions and continue to treat her as if she were a child. In a burst of healthy independence, Rita started a relationship with Charlie, also in his forties, whom she met through an Internet dating service. They were both thrilled to find each other and, after dating for about six months, decided to get married. Rita's parents strongly objected. They disapproved of Charlie and continued to exert pressure on Rita to do things their way.

Today, Rita's new marriage is close to collapse because of her continued dependency on her parents. Rita feels torn between her love for Charlie and her loyalty to them. She tries hard to please everyone but is finding it impossible. Rita feels hopeless as she slides into anxiety and depression.

Rita's parents believe they love her, but their love is smothering her instead of freeing her to live as an adult woman. Even if Rita's parents never recognize the effects of their behavior or change their ways, Rita can break free. She will have to acknowledge her dependence as destructive to her marriage and to her maturity as a person, and she will need to learn to stand on her own two feet with her husband. If she refuses to take these steps, her marriage will likely be destroyed by her parents' interference and Rita's inability to separate from them. In addition, Rita will never grow into the adult woman God intended. She will remain immature.

Terri and John, Tom and his pastor, and Rita and her parents are all in destructive relationships. Much of the way they relate to one another feels normal to them. They don't consider themselves abusive people or victims of an abusive relationship, yet the personal and relational damage is obvious.

If you find yourself in a similar situation, the good news is that there are some things you can do to recognize, identify, and stop destructive relationship patterns. With God's help, I believe that change, growth, and healing are possible for you. First, we need to name what's wrong, because you can't begin to change what you do not (or will not) see.

Is Your Relationship Difficult or Destructive?

No one is in any meaningful relationship very long without experiencing some pain. Pain is not proof of a bad relationship or even a harmful one. There is no perfect relationship or perfect person. Ever since Eve's decision to listen to the serpent's voice instead of trusting God, paradise has been lost. The consequences are sin and brokenness for everyone.

Each one of us has the potential to be destructive or sometimes abusive. Who hasn't in a flash of anger done or said something deeply regrettable? When my son, Ryan, was about two years old, he flung himself down in the middle of a store, kicking and screaming because I wouldn't buy him a toy he wanted. Embarrassed and angry, I grabbed his arm and yanked him to his feet. His crying only intensified as he hollered loud enough for the entire store to hear that I broke his arm. Everyone's eyes turned to me, and Ryan's arm dangled limply by his side.

Horrified, I rushed him to the emergency room, crying and confessing my wrongdoing to the doctor. Fortunately, Ryan's arm was not broken. Instead I learned about "nursemaid elbow," which occurs when a young child's elbow joint is dislocated when pulled too hard. Although I never yanked Ryan to his feet again, his elbow accidentally dislocated several more times during his childhood.

Because of sin, all of us make poor choices at times and have sinful reactions to life's frustrations and hurts. But when we see we have been dishonest, disrespectful, unkind, or harsh with someone, we have the opportunity to admit it, apologize, and make necessary repairs to the relationship. We understand we have hurt someone, and we don't make excuses for our bad behavior by blaming the other person for what we did. We genuinely feel remorse for causing someone to suffer and make sincere efforts not to repeat the same behavior in the future.

That being the case, how can we tell whether our relationships are relatively healthy, if sometimes difficult (including sin and pain as well as mutual repentance and forgiveness), or unhealthy and destructive?

As I've just suggested, a single episode of sinful behavior does not usually constitute a destructive relationship. Pervasive and repetitive patterns of actions and attitudes that result in tearing someone down or inhibiting a person's growth, however, do. A destructive relationship is not the same thing as a difficult one. Learning calculus is difficult, but it leads to growth and to greater intellectual or mathematical maturity. On the other hand, ingesting cyanide is destructive. It harms and often leads to death.

Hurtful attitudes and actions can be exhibited in a variety of different ways within a relationship, such as by consistently treating someone with indifference, neglect, disrespect, cruelty, deception, or harshness. These destructive patterns are often accompanied by the perpetrator's lack of personal awareness, accountability, and genuine remorse. The perpetrator does not experience empathy for the suffering they've caused the other person because, in his or her mind, that person is at fault or responsible for the problem.

You might find it difficult to identify destructive relational styles, especially if your childhood contained similar elements. Many of us are not even aware that the way we interact with someone or the way we have been treated *is* destructive. It feels normal. It may even feel like love. However, like termites silently invading a home, over time the evidence of destruction becomes undeniable.

Five Relationship Patterns That Are Always Destructive

Over the years, I have identified five distinct types of harmful relationships. As you read through this list, you might find that your relationship with someone contains all five characteristics, or you may identify with only one or two. Please understand that if you experience even one of these patterns consistently in your relationship with someone, the behavior will cause harm to both you and your relationship if left unaddressed.

WHEN DOES A RELATIONSHIP BECOME DESTRUCTIVE?

1. One or both parties commit physical, emotional, verbal, or sexual abuse upon the other. (See "Categories of Abuse" at the back of this book.)

2. One person is regularly overprotective, overbearing, or both toward the other.

3. One person is overdependent upon the other to affirm his or her personal value and worth, to meet all of his or her needs, and to make most of his or her decisions.

4. One person demonstrates a pattern of deceiving the other through lying, hiding, pretending, misleading, or twisting information to make something appear other than what it is.

5. One person exhibits chronic indifference, neglect, or both toward the thoughts, feelings, or well-being of the other.

Remember, because we are all sinners, we are all capable of doing each of these things. What makes these sinful interactions destructive is their repetitive pattern, as well as lack of awareness, lack of remorse, and lack of significant change. This distinction should not minimize the sinfulness and destructiveness of isolated instances. There are times when a single incident of abuse or serious deceit is all it takes to completely destroy a relationship, even if the offender is remorseful and desires to change. It only takes one bullet to kill someone.

Let's look a little more closely at why each of these five interpersonal styles is so toxic.

Abuse

Not every destructive relationship involves abuse, but any relationship that entails any kind of abuse is always destructive. When diagnosing the problem of relational abuse, there are important distinctions between relationships in which one person continually seeks power over the other and uses abusive tactics (whether physical, verbal, sexual, or economic) to control and intimidate, mutually abusive behavior (where both partners verbally or physically assault each other out of anger and frustration), and one-time abusive incidents (like my arm-pulling episode with Ryan).

Fear of being physically, sexually, or emotionally harmed squashes all healthy communication. When afraid, it is impossible for anyone to honestly express thoughts or feelings, to disagree, or to be different. Power-seeking abusers don't love their victims in a godly way. The abusers' focus is only on *their* feelings, *their* wants, *their* needs, and *their* preferences. Their victims function merely as objects that can help to fulfill those desires, wishes, needs, and so on.

When an abuser fails to attain these goals, rage often results. The volatile response is both a punishment (the relationship partner has not met expectations) and a stern warning not to fall short again. The abuser learns that rage works. It is an extremely effective way to control someone.

Men and women both use rage to control others, although men are more statistically prone to physical and sexual abuse than women are. Most of the time, abusive relationships are confined to intimate partnerships such as dating, live-in, or marriage. But at times the imbalance of power and control can be seen between adult children and elderly parents, church leaders and their con-gregations, or in places of employment. Emotional ties, economic dependence, and (in marriage) biblical mandates against divorce keep many individuals feeling trapped and helpless. They have no idea how to change the balance of power.

In contrast to an abusive relationship where one person seeks power over another, abusive attitudes and behaviors can occur in any relationship when one or both individuals cannot manage the frustrations of life or their tempers in a mature and godly way. The apostle Paul warns us against this kind of interaction: "If you are always biting and devouring one another, watch out! Beware of destroying one another" (Galatians 5:15).

Phil and Joanne have been married for over 30 years. Most of those years have been a disappointment. Neither one feels loved, respected, or valued by the other. They stay together because God hates divorce (Malachi 2:16), but emotionally they divorced years ago. Their best communication is functional (they can impart information to one another), but their regular communication is destructive. Joanne's pattern is to verbally attack, demean, and humiliate her husband. Phil withdraws and distances himself until he can't take it anymore, and then he explodes. Both Phil and

Joanne profess to be Christians, yet each regularly sins against the other. They justify their behavior in their own minds, citing their pain and disappointment. Each wants the other to change first.

There is hope for Phil and Joanne's relationship, but not until they both admit that their legitimate desires for a better spouse have blinded them to their own destructive patterns. Until they love and pursue God more than they love and pursue their own desires, they will continue to make excuses and avoid taking responsibility for their destructive and sinful interactions.

The important difference between this kind of mutually abusive pattern and oppressive abuse is that Phil does not try to micro-manage Joanne or gain dominance over her. She has plenty of decision-making power within their relationship, as does he. But when either of them becomes disappointed and angry with the other, both turn destructive. If left to escalate, mutually abusive attitudes and actions can be just as lethal to the overall safety and well-being of the people in the relationship. The underlying dynamics and solutions, however, are different from those of an abusive relationship in which power and control issues are central. When we get to part 2, this will be an important distinction.

A one-time abusive incident may suggest one person's attempt to gain power and control over another, like my effort to gain control over Ryan and his tantrum, but the abuser usually quickly repents, and the action is not likely to recur.

Overprotection and Overbearingness

A step down from the abusive relationship that I described above is a kind of controlling relationship in which there is a consistent pattern of giving advice, making decisions for another person, or telling someone how to act, all under the guise of "I know what's best for you or what's best for us." This might include telling someone what to wear, how to cook, which television programs are permissible, and how often to visit family and friends. Sometimes the controlling behavior is limited to specific areas in the relationship, such as decisions related to money or friends.

John and Terri, the couple I introduced at the beginning of this chapter, fit this pattern. John was overbearing toward Terri but did not use verbally abusive language or force to secure Terri's compliance. If Terri had been firmer in the beginning of their relationship, things might have evolved differently between them.

What made John and Terri's relationship destructive was the combination of John's overbearing personality, his belief that his ways were always best, Terri's lack of confidence in herself, and her natural desire to please others. Had Terri confronted John's superior attitude and take-charge behavior early in their marriage, he might have backed down and learned to encourage rather than try to change Terri. He also might have developed more humility and tolerance of her differences. (On the other hand, John might have escalated his control, turning to more abusive tactics to gain more control and power over Terri.)

All of us who are parents have been tempted at times to become overbearing or overprotective toward our children. But when such a high level of involvement becomes a regular pattern, especially as children get older, it hampers their growth and maturity. It's true: We hate to see our children hurt or make a mistake, but when we take on what they should be learning or doing for themselves, we harm them. Today, more and more adult children continue to depend on their parents because they have not learned how to stand on their own two feet.

Overdependence

Dependent behavior typically occurs in unhealthy parent–child relationships like that of Rita and her parents. This pattern also occurs in adult friendships or in marriages when one person leans too heavily upon a friend or partner to make decisions, to be continuously available, and to meet all emotional and relational needs.

Jane and Marcy met at women's Bible study and were soon feeling like best friends. Single and lonely, Jane felt God had finally answered her prayers for a kindred-spirit girlfriend. Marcy had many other friends but felt a special draw to Jane. She knew what it was like to feel lonely, and her heart went out to Jane. Before long, Jane was calling Marcy every night. They talked for hours. Jane always hung up telling Marcy how much she liked her and enjoyed their friendship.

Marcy loved that Jane was so affirming of their friendship. She liked Jane too, but before long she began to notice that whenever she had something else she wanted to do, Jane expressed hurt feelings. Jane also insinuated that Marcy should include her in all of her other activities and felt angry whenever she discovered Marcy went someplace without her. Jane needed Marcy's friendship, and she felt rejected and furious when Marcy wasn't always available for her.

At first Marcy felt flattered to be so needed, but after a while Jane's expectations became burdensome and tiring. Jane's dependence on Marcy was unhealthy. She expected Marcy to fill her emotional void and leaned on her so heavily that Marcy began to distance herself in order to protect her personal boundaries. Jane got hurt, Marcy burned out, and their relationship eventually ended.

If you recognize that you are overly dependent upon people, or if you find yourself regularly inviting or attracting people to depend on you, understand that God did not intend for people to continuously depend on other people for their well-being. As we mature, he wants us to depend upon him. Certainly God uses individuals to meet many of our needs, but no one person can meet all our needs all the time. When we believe we always need a particular someone, we put that person in God's position in our lives. Replacing God with a person will destroy us.

In the same vein, it's possible to put others in God's position by giving them the power to determine your worth and value. You might be a natural people pleaser who is captured by the fear of man (Proverbs 29:25). Most people want to be liked and valued by others, but when our entire well-being is dependent upon whether we are liked, loved, accepted, or valued by a particular person or group, we have allowed an unhealthy dependence to take root.

Lying

Carmen and Diane were becoming close friends when Carmen began noticing inconsistencies in what Diane said. Carmen caught her in some lies. Once, when Carmen knew Diane had not been honest, she gently confronted her friend. Diane reacted defensively and denied it. Carmen didn't argue but instead began distancing herself from Diane. Although she remained polite and friendly, she no longer considered Diane a close friend. Carmen didn't trust her. Diane's deceit and denial didn't destroy Carmen, but it did destroy their friendship.

In another situation, Cindy came to me for counseling, depressed and angry with herself over the breakup of her marriage. Her husband's secretary was pregnant with his child, and he wanted to divorce Cindy and marry his lover. For years Cindy had suspected that Gary was involved with his secretary, but Gary adamantly denied it. When Cindy would question how much time he spent with the woman after work hours, Gary managed explanations that sounded reasonable, even acceptable, and Cindy ended up feeling ashamed for even questioning him.

Other times, when Cindy would confront Gary with something she observed, he'd gently put his arm around her and tell her in a kind tone that what she saw didn't actually happen. Cindy began to think she was imagining things.[1] She left those confrontations feeling horribly guilty for questioning Gary, especially after he swore to her over and over that nothing was going on. Now she felt like a fool.

Gary's pattern of deceit not only destroyed their relationship, it eroded Cindy's confidence in her own perceptions and thoughts.

She had begun to suspect that she was either terribly insecure or crazy, when in fact she was right all along.

We lie not only when we contradict the truth, but also when we mislead someone's thinking. We lie when we pretend things are fine, when in reality we are angry or unhappy. We lie when we hide a problem with drinking or Internet pornography or other sin, making excuses and throwing up smokescreens that cover our tracks.

We even lie to ourselves when we make something bad look acceptable, or even desirable. I've heard some Christians defend a husband who demands his own way by explaining that he's exercising headship, when in reality he's practicing selfishness. Our culture is adept at using the power of language to mislead and warp perceptions. We call teacher–student sexual relations "affairs" instead of abuse of power. We call the brutal killing of a woman "a crime of passion" as the perpetrator sobs, "I loved her so much." Language is twisted to make our actions look less heinous, more acceptable. But the Bible warns us, "What sorrow for those who say that evil is good and good is evil, that dark is light and light is dark, that bitter is sweet and sweet is bitter" (Isaiah 5:20).

Lying is one of the most destructive things we can do when we're confronted about something we've done wrong (Proverbs 26:18-19,28). I have witnessed marriage after marriage crumble because the person who has been challenged will not come clean through humble confession of the whole truth. Sheila discovered George was having an affair with someone at church. He broke down, admitted it, and seemingly repented. But he didn't tell Sheila that the woman was pregnant. George secretly arranged for her to leave the church and plan an adoption. When the whole truth came out (and it usually does), the trust that Sheila began to rebuild with George disintegrated and was impossible to restore.

Indifference and Neglect

Anna begged her husband to stay home with her and the kids after work and on weekends, but soccer always came first. He spent two nights a week and many weekends with the guys, playing soccer, talking soccer, refereeing soccer, and watching soccer on TV. Anna felt like a single parent carrying the entire responsibility for the household. She also felt lonely. John enjoyed soccer and his friends much more than he seemed to enjoy her. She believed he saw her as someone there to cook, clean, pay the bills, wash his clothes, take care of the kids, and provide sex when he wanted it. Anna questioned whether he ever thought about what she needed or wanted. Was she important to him as a person, or was she merely a caregiver who met his felt needs?

From time to time in every marriage or close relationship, it's quite normal for one person to feel like the other isn't sharing the load. It's true—sometimes the burden is unequal. The question we need to ask ourselves isn't, *Am I giving more?* but, *Is there a habitual pattern of disregard for my felt needs, desires, feelings, goals, or perspectives?* If the answer is yes, then we need to learn to speak up so that this pattern changes. Otherwise, instead of being mutually caring, the relationship will turn into a one-sided ministry, or deteriorate and end.

Recently while I was counseling a woman, she asked me how long she should continue a friendship in which the other person never reciprocated. My client felt weary of carrying the entire friendship. She always had to initiate contact and plan time together. Her friend would often cancel their plans at the last minute and rarely rescheduled. I said, "It sounds like your friend isn't all that interested in maintaining your friendship. Why don't you talk with her about it and see if you can make it better? Or perhaps you will agree that the friendship has fizzled out."

Whenever we are in a relationship with someone, we expect it to be characterized by certain qualities that enable it to function and flourish. The basics are caring, honesty, and respect. Like Jane, sometimes our expectations of another person may be unrealistic, and our demands upon them will become destructive to the relationship. However, a healthy relationship requires effort. Like everything else in life, what we don't maintain deteriorates.

When we are chronically indifferent or neglectful toward someone, we effectively say, "I don't care about you," or, "You don't mean enough to me to deserve my time and resources." Because we're not God and have limited resources of time and energy, we can't commit to be in close relationships with lots of people, but those we have committed ourselves to expect some of our time, attention, and resources in order to feel cared about. When we make an implied or stated commitment to someone, then behave in a way that indicates indifference to the person's needs, the person will feel confused and devalued.

Lucy suffered a miscarriage early in her pregnancy. Devastated, she turned to her husband, Allen, for support. Lucy cried, "He turned his back on me and went to sleep. I felt so hurt and unloved. It was like our baby and I didn't exist."

If a healthy mutual relationship with someone is impossible, don't simply give up. God calls us to love always, and that includes our enemies; however, God never commands us to have close relationships with them. In parts 2 and 3 I'll cover what loving our enemies looks like and how to do it.

Another way we can identify what's wrong with relationships is by observing what's right in thriving relationships. Bankers receive special training to spot counterfeit money by inspecting thousands of genuine bills. Medical students diagnose disease by studying healthy bodies. The best way to recognize unhealthy or destructive relationship patterns is to compare and contrast them with the characteristics that describe healthy relationships.

Foundational Elements Necessary for Relationships to Flourish

People engage in many different kinds of relationships. We have professional relationships, business friendships, and casual connections with neighbors across the fence and with folks at church. On a deeper level, we have close friends, best friends, romantic friends, and family ties with our siblings, children, parents, in-laws, and spouses. In each of these relationships there are different expectations for how much honesty, commitment, support, and time will be required for the relationship to be mutually beneficial. Even so, the most casual or superficial relationship can deteriorate into a destructive encounter if the following foundational elements are devalued by one or both people trying to make the relationship work.

Let's look at the basic qualities necessary for any relationship to flourish in a healthy way.

Commitment and Care

In all healthy relationships, personal or professional, the well-being of the other person is important to us even when we're mad, tired, or busy. At its most basic level, commitment promises that the other person's feelings, desires, needs, wants, and thoughts will matter to us, and that when the person considers something urgent or important, we give it our attention. This doesn't always mean we have to do what the person wants. We don't even necessarily have to feel the same way about an issue, but at least we give it proper thought.

Some people are legally married but uncommitted to their spouses' nurture, support, or welfare. This consistent disregard for a partner's thoughts, feelings, and well-being creates significant emotional distress, because the promise of commitment and expectation of care is clearly part of the marital covenant.

Genuine caring values the other person's happiness, well-being, and goodness. Selfish love is only interested in what the other person has to contribute to the relationship.

Honesty and Integrity

Personal honesty (not lying to yourself) and interpersonal honesty (as appropriate for the level of intimacy in the relationship) are crucial for trust to flourish. Not all relationships require full transparency (in other words, keep your emotional clothes on unless the relationship is intimate), but all relationships thrive on authenticity. Others deserve to see who you really are. I love that I can be myself with my husband. He knows my good side and my immature side, and although he may not like certain parts of me, he accepts me.

As I said earlier, pretending, denying, hiding, evading, shading, or twisting facts or your feelings to create a particular impression are forms of lying and will lead to mistrust. Like acid on metal, deceit erodes the foundations necessary to support a healthy relationship.

Honesty isn't the same as blurting out everything we feel at the moment of its greatest intensity—that can be very destructive. Healthy individuals know it's wise to contain their toxic emotions until they have some time to think through their feelings and pray about how to approach the problem constructively. People who exercise restraint can be more certain that their actions will lead to healing and restoration rather than mere relief or a descending spiral of anger.

Mutual Respect

All people, no matter how much we might dislike them or disagree with their beliefs or behaviors, contain within them the precious image of God. Christians should never mock, disdain, or disrespect an individual (Proverbs 14:21) even if they disapprove of the person's actions.

It is so easy to show our disapproval of people with disrespect. We roll our eyes, snicker at their feelings or thoughts, mock them, show disgust or contempt, make degrading comments, gossip about them, humiliate them publicly, or continually try to change them into the person we think they should be.

Healthy adult relationships exist where both people in the relationship give and both receive. David and Michelle didn't have a perfect marriage, but they certainly had a happy one. They loved each other, and others readily observed their caring. People who knew them well saw that they mutually shared power and responsibility in their home. They both practiced sacrifice and submission for the good and welfare of each other and their children. Together they valued an open exchange of ideas, feelings, and thoughts in their family, and they considered everyone's perspective important. Not only was there room for mutual love, encouragement, and caring, but there was also freedom to respectfully challenge, confront, and strengthen one another.

Jesus modeled these kinds of interactions for us, showing us a picture of good mental, emotional, and spiritual health. Except for Christ, however, no person is always right or sees everything accurately all of the time. I am deeply concerned by those who discourage Christian wives from ever challenging their husbands, even when it looks like a man is driving himself or the entire family straight off a cliff. This kind of teaching is destructive, not only to the wife, who must lie to her husband in order to not wound his ego, but also to the husband, who believes he's doing well when in reality he's not (Proverbs 29:1; Galatians 6:1; James 5:19-20). Each person in the relationship is harmed, a healthy marriage is impossible, and the children observe and absorb destructive relationship patterns only to repeat them in their adult lives.

Are You in an Emotionally Destructive Relationship?

If you think that a relationship you are in may be destructive or heading that way, ask yourself the following questions. Your answers to these questions will help you look at the health of one or more of your relationships and see the particular patterns that are destructive. Be honest with yourself. I understand that it can be extremely difficult to face the hard truth that something is wrong. Like one of my clients, you might even tell yourself, "I'd rather not know, because if I know, then I have to do something about it, and I don't know what to do." You can't fix or change something if you are not willing to look at it truthfully. Don't turn back now. There is a part of you that already knows it's time to face what's wrong and to learn what you need to change, or you wouldn't have picked up this book. Remember, God sees you, and he is with you.

Some people realize that they are in several bad relationships at the same time or have had a string of destructive friendships or marriages. Complete this questionnaire once for each relationship you are concerned about. For example, if you're evaluating your relationship with your spouse, answer each question about your spouse first. Don't combine answers about your spouse with answers about another relationship. You can apply the questionnaire to each of your relationships. It will help you not only identify whether your relationships are destructive, but in what way they are destructive.

1. Does the person use physical force or threats of force to make you do something you don't want to do or to keep you from doing something you want to do?	Never Seldom Sometimes Frequently Almost Always
2. Does the person use verbal weapons such as cursing, name calling, degrading comments, constant criticism, or blaming to get you to do something you don't want to do or to keep you from doing something you want to do?	Never Seldom Sometimes Frequently Almost Always
3. Does the person curse at you, call you names, humiliate you in public, or degrade you when he or she is unhappy with something you do?	Never Seldom Sometimes Frequently Almost Always

4. Does the person force or manipulate you to perform sexually in ways you do not want to?	<u>Never</u>　　Seldom　　Sometimes Frequently　　Almost Always		

5. Do you ever feel afraid of the person?

Never　　Seldom　　<u>Sometimes</u>
Frequently　　Almost Always

6. Does the person yell, scream, curse, or hurt you physically when he or she is frustrated or angry?

Never　　Seldom　　<u>Sometimes</u>
Frequently　　Almost Always

7. Does the person threaten to alienate your children from you or use them to intimidate you into giving in to what he or she wants?

<u>Never</u>　　Seldom　　Sometimes
Frequently　　Almost Always

8. Are you afraid to disagree with the person?

Never　　<u>Seldom</u>　　Sometimes
Frequently　　Almost Always

9. When you share your thoughts and feelings about something important to you, does the person ignore you, make fun of you, or dismiss you?

Never　　Seldom　　<u>Sometimes</u>
Frequently　　Almost Always

10. Are you verbally or physically abusive, or both, toward the person?

Never　　Seldom　　Sometimes
<u>Frequently</u>　　Almost Always

11. Does the person always think he or she is right to the point of arguing with you until you concede or give up?

Never　　Seldom　　Sometimes
Frequently　　<u>Almost Always</u>

12. Does the person make most of your decisions for you?

Never　　Seldom　　<u>Sometimes</u>
Frequently　　Almost Always

13. Does the person control the family money, giving you little or no say?	Never	Seldom	Sometimes
	Frequently	Almost Always	

14. Have you given up things that were important to you because the person pressured you?	Never	Seldom	<u>Sometimes</u>
	Frequently	Almost Always	

15. Does the person pout or withdraw from you for extended periods of time when he or she is angry or upset with you?	Never	Seldom	Sometimes
	Frequently	<u>Almost Always</u>	

16. When you ask for a time-out or don't want to talk about something anymore, does the person keep badgering you to engage?	Never	Seldom	<u>Sometimes</u>
	Frequently	Almost Always	

17. Does the person lie to you?	Never	Seldom	Sometimes
	<u>Frequently</u>	Almost Always	

18. Have you observed the person lying to others?	Never	Seldom	<u>Sometimes</u>
	Frequently	Almost Always	

19. Does the person tell you something didn't happen, when you know it did?	Never	Seldom	<u>Sometimes</u>
	Frequently	Almost Always	

20. Does the person question or challenge your certainty of what he or she said or did?	Never	Seldom	<u>Sometimes</u>
	Frequently	Almost Always	

21. Does the person depend on you to meet all his or her needs?	<u>Never</u>	Seldom	Sometimes
	Frequently	Almost Always	

22. Do you feel more like a child than an adult in the relationship?	Never	Seldom	<u>Sometimes</u>
	Frequently	Almost Always	

23. Are you emotionally devastated when the person is upset with you or doesn't want to be in relationship with you?

    Never   Seldom   Sometimes   Frequently   <u>Almost Always</u>

24. When you try to talk with the person about your feelings or something that's bothering you, do you end up feeling like the trouble is entirely your fault?

    Never   Seldom   Sometimes   Frequently   <u>Almost Always</u>

25. When the person does something wrong, does he or she blame you or anyone else for it?

    Never   Seldom   Sometimes   <u>Frequently</u>   Almost Always

26. Does the other person make excuses for his or her behavior (anger, jealousy, lies)?

    Never   Seldom   Sometimes   Frequently   <u>Almost Always</u>

27. Do you feel loved and cared for in the relationship?

    <u>Never</u>   Seldom   Sometimes   Frequently   Almost Always

28. Can you safely express an opinion that is different from the person's?

    Never   Seldom   <u>Sometimes</u>   Frequently   Almost Always

29. Does the person show interest in you and your needs?

    <u>Never</u>   Seldom   Sometimes   Frequently   Almost Always

30. Are you able to express your honest thoughts and feelings with the person?

    <u>Never</u>   Seldom   Sometimes   Frequently   Almost Always

31. When the person does something wrong, does he or she admit it and take responsibility for it?

    Never   <u>Seldom</u>   Sometimes   Frequently   Almost Always

If you answered any question up through question 26 with anything other than *never,* you are likely in an unhealthy relationship.

If you answered most questions with *sometimes, frequently,* or *almost always,* you are definitely in a destructive and likely an abusive relationship. Now go back and look at which questions in particular you answered with any answer other than *never.*

Questions 1–16 describe the main characteristics of an abusive relationship where the abuser's desire for power and control is at the root. If answering this questionnaire has revealed to you that you are in an abusive relationship, please seek appropriate help from those in your church or community who are experts in helping victims of abusive relationships. (You will find information about various resources at the back of the book.) If you answered *seldom* to any question in this group, you still may be in danger, depending upon the severity of the abuse. Once a year is seldom, but it is still too often in a long-term relationship such as a marriage.

Question 10 looks in particular for patterns of mutual abuse. If you answered this question with *frequently* or *almost always,* then your relationship might be more mutually abusive. Review questions 1–16 and ask them about yourself. Are you engaging in the same abusive behaviors that you cite in the other person?

Questions 11–17 reflect less obvious ways in which the relationship may be controlling. That does not mean it is not abusive, but if you answered *never* to questions 1–9, you may be in a controlling relationship that is not obviously abusive.

Questions 17–20 describe a relationship where deceit is present. If most of your answers reflect problems in this area, your relationship is built on lies and it is unstable. You cannot trust someone who does not tell you the truth. And without trust, no relationship can endure.

Questions 21–23 describe a relationship that is overdependent.

Questions 24–26 describe a person who does not take personal responsibility for behavior or wrongdoing.

Stop here and name some of the specific destructive elements in your relationship with this particular person. Is there physical, verbal, or sexual abuse? How about controlling behaviors and attitudes? Is there more mutual abuse? Are you too dependent? Is there deceit or a lack of personal accountability or responsibility?

Questions 27–31 describe the basic elements of a healthy relationship. If you answered *never* or *seldom* to any of these questions, your answers indicate that your relationship is unhealthy and probably destructive.

Right now you may feel overwhelmed and frightened. These feelings are normal for anyone facing difficult truths. If you want to become healthier and have better relationships, I want to assure you that you can begin working on your part. The rest of this book, especially chapters 6 through 12, will show you how.

When my septic system backed into my basement, I wanted to close my eyes and pretend that it wasn't happening. Then I wanted to move out. Instead, that evening I cleaned up what I could and told myself that washing everything with bleach was good enough. This approach would certainly be a lot easier than ripping apart my entire basement. However, when I consulted with professionals who knew better, they assured me that the bacteria would not be removed with bleach alone. It needed a more drastic approach.

I don't want to scare you, but it's important that you understand the serious consequences of destructive relationships so that you will do all you can to change these patterns. I know, it feels easier to simply close your eyes or try to get by, hoping that the damage won't be too bad, but trust me: Ignoring destruction doesn't ever make it better or even neutral. The damage only grows.

God never minimizes the destructiveness that someone's sin can have upon another person. Sin destroys. Let's look at the effects that destructive relationships have on our bodies, our minds, our emotions, our spirits, our children, and our personhood.

2

The Consequences of an Emotionally Destructive Relationship

Yelling at living things does tend to kill the spirit in them.
Sticks and stones may break our bones,
but words will break our hearts.

ROBERT FULGHUM

The human spirit can endure a sick body,
but who can bear a crushed spirit?

PROVERBS 18:14

⁓

Stacy loved people and excelled in high school and college. After graduation, she was accepted to medical school and, after years of hard work, fulfilled her dream to become a physician. While still an intern, Stacy married her high-school sweetheart, Stan. Each of them was so busy establishing their respective careers that neither paid much attention to nurturing their relationship. But after things settled down and they had more time for one another, Stacy noticed that Stan preferred working on his computer over spending time with her. When she spoke to him, he rarely responded positively. Her efforts to draw him into conversation fell on deaf ears and often elicited a cutting or demeaning remark like "Quit nagging me."

Over the years, their marriage didn't change, but Stacy did. Her outgoing, fun-loving personality began to die. She became critical and sullen. "If that's the way he wants to be," she said, "two can play this game." Stacy ignored Stan. She refused to engage him and called him names like *relationally retarded* and *loser*. Stan responded with his own digs and withdrew further from Stacy. Stacy felt like she hated her husband, but perhaps more surprising, she realized she hated herself.

She cried, "This marriage is turning me into someone I don't want to be, someone I don't even like."

We Are Influenced and Affected by Other People

Recent research in brain science confirms what the Bible tells us: God has designed humans to be social creatures, hardwired to connect. Well-known psychologist Daniel Goleman, in his book *Social Intelligence: The New Science of Human Relationships*, says,

> Neuroscience has discovered that our brain's very design makes it sociable, inexorably drawn into an intimate brain-to-brain linkup whenever we engage with another person. That neural bridge lets us affect the brain—and so the body—of everyone we interact with, just as they do us.[1]

The Bible states that people powerfully influence us, both positively and negatively. In Stacy's marriage, Stan's negativity and indifference impacted Stacy far more than she realized. His behavior diminished their marital happiness, and she unintentionally allowed it to shape her into someone she didn't like or respect.[2]

While in college, I lived in a dorm where cursing and profanity were the norm. After a while, I found myself thinking (and sometimes using) bad words when frustrated, even though I hated them. Please don't misunderstand what I'm saying. No one *made* me curse. Nor did Stan's indifference toward Stacy *make* her sullen and critical. Though we are not controlled by another person's actions, we are still affected by the company we keep.

God warns us to be careful about the friends we choose (Proverbs 12:26). For example, he cautions us not to associate with angry people lest we become like them (Proverbs 22:24-25), and that socializing with violent people will take us down destructive paths (Proverbs 1:10-15; 16:29). The apostle Paul tells us that bad company corrupts good morals (1 Corinthians 15:33). By the same token, God's Word also says that when we befriend wise people, we too will grow in wisdom (Proverbs 13:20).

People don't merely influence our behavior and our character; they can also impact our overall well-being. Brad returned to graduate school at the urging of his company and earned his MBA with honors. His supervisor recognized his potential and told him he was a candidate for higher management positions. After graduation, Brad received a promotion, new responsibilities, and a new boss. Eager to please and wanting to make a good impression, Brad embraced his new job with vigor and worked extra hours and many weekends. His new boss, however, seemed unimpressed with Brad's efforts. She often criticized and demeaned Brad and his work, leaving him with a funny feeling that she saw Brad as incompetent and certainly not higher-level-management material.

Over the next few months, Brad started getting severe headaches. He also began drinking a couple of glasses of wine at night, "Just to relax," he said. Brad snapped more at his wife and children, and though he once possessed confidence, he now found himself second-guessing his judgment.

"Leslie," he said, "I don't feel like myself. I'm as nervous as a cat, I feel afraid to make decisions at work, and when I do I make stupid mistakes. I've never had these problems before. What's wrong with me?"

Brad's problem isn't a psychological problem; it's an interpersonal one. His boss's chronic negativity and cutting remarks have undermined Brad's self-confidence and affected his well-being.

For both Brad and Stacy, as well as the rest of us, gaining awareness of this powerful interpersonal process is the first step in countering its lethal effects. Destructive relationships profoundly affect our emotional, physical, mental, relational, and spiritual health.

Emotional Effects

Sometimes the first sign that you are in a destructive relationship isn't seen, it is felt. Terri felt like she was dying inside. She could not put her finger on what was wrong with her relationship with her husband, John, but she knew it was killing her. Others feel depressed, chronically guilty, numb, exhausted, angry, unloved, unimportant, devalued, or dismissed.

Our emotions function like a relational Geiger counter. As they make noise, they signal to us that something is wrong. Terri told me, "I feel like I'm suffocating in this relationship. I'm afraid to cause any waves. When I do, it's like spiking the cat's fur in the wrong direction, and then it won't lie back down." Brad said, "I feel so squashed. My boss always has the upper hand."

Don't misunderstand. Feeling emotional pain does not necessarily mean you're in a destructive relationship. We all experience some hurt in every relationship, and pain is often part of our growth process. Recently, my husband shared with me that he thought I was getting too absorbed in my own life, needs, and feelings. He found a kind way to say, "You're getting a little full of yourself." No one likes to hear that, but I needed an attitude adjustment, and I was thankful he loved me enough to tell me the truth. But his hard words were nested in the context of our relationship patterns of caring, commitment, honesty, and respect, which made that particularly difficult pill of truth go down a little easier (although not without a hard gulp). Proverbs reminds us that "wounds from a friend can be trusted" (Proverbs 27:6 NIV). There are times when hearing hard truth grieves our feelings or, more likely, wounds our egos.

Here's a good rule of thumb: If you're in a relationship that lacks mutual caring, safety, honesty, or respect, *and* you regularly feel anxiety, fear, shame, anger, or despair, then your emotions are warning you that you are in a destructive relationship. Even if you sometimes experience positive feelings toward this person and are able to have good times together, chronic dread, fear, anger, or stress quench whatever positive feelings you have.

Emotions are contagious. As children, my younger sister Patt and I always got into trouble because once one of us started giggling, the other couldn't help giggling too, even if we had no idea what was so funny. Likewise, living with someone who typically emits negativity and harsh words makes one extremely vulnerable to feeling pessimistic and negative.

Daniel Goleman says, "When someone dumps their toxic feelings on us—explodes in anger or threats, shows disgust or contempt—they activate in us circuitry for those very same distressing emotions."[3] Don't underestimate the immediate or long-term consequences of living with chronic relational duress. When we fail (or are unable) to take effective action on behalf of our own emotional distress, we feel helpless. Over time, we start to believe we're powerless to change anything.

We need to be careful not to think that our emotions are separate from the rest of our lives. Brad suffered severe headaches as well as increased anger and a loss of self-esteem. His relationship with his boss spilled over at home in the ways he treated his wife and children. A destructive relationship impacts all facets of life.

Physical Effects

In a destructive relationship, our body suffers as well as our emotions. Terri's depression led to endless fatigue, insomnia, gastrointestinal difficulties, and autoimmune problems, which gave her frequent colds and flu-like symptoms as she continually swallowed her anger and stifled her personhood in order to live peaceably under John's rule.

Research undeniably demonstrates strong links between our relationships and our physical health, as Goleman writes:

> Our social interactions operate as modulators, something like interpersonal thermostats that continually reset key aspects of our brain function as they orchestrate our emotions.
>
> The resulting feelings have far-reaching consequences that ripple throughout our body, sending out cascades of hormones that regulate biological systems from our heart to our immune cells. Perhaps most astonishing, science now tracks connections between the most stressful relationships and the operation of specific genes that regulate the immune system.
>
> To a surprising extent, then, our relationships mold not just our experience but our biology...
>
> That link is a double-edged sword: nourishing relationships have a beneficial impact on our health, while toxic ones can act like slow poison in our bodies.[4]

We think foolishly when we believe that we can remain in destructive relationships and stay immune to its toxic physical effects. Studies demonstrate that destructive interpersonal conflict (for example, arguments that are characterized by sarcasm, demeaning comments, and nastiness) not only break our hearts, they clog our arteries.[5]

In an interview with the Web site WebMD, Mimi Guarneri, a cardiologist and author of the book *The Heart Speaks: A Cardiologist Reveals the Secret Language of the Heart,* said, "We know that when we're angry, our bodies are surging with stress hormones that raise our blood pressure, heart rate, and stress hormone levels."[6]

We are fearfully and wonderfully made (Psalm 149:14 NIV). God has wired us so that when we experience upsetting emotions, they signal the body to release particular chemicals into the bloodstream. This is a good thing. It empowers us to fight or flee in order to get out of danger. However, when we are chronically upset and our bodies regularly dump these chemicals into the bloodstream, we put ourselves at risk for greater physical and emotional problems. Anxiety, high blood pressure, migraine headaches, depression, addictions, gastrointestinal disturbances, and chronic fatigue are just a few of the physical–emotional problems I've observed as I've worked with individuals in destructive relationships. That is one reason why God tells us that even if we are unable to resolve interpersonal conflict, we personally need to let go of our own anger before the end of each day (Ephesians 4:26).

God's Word also encourages us: as we gain wisdom and live as God tells us to, our bodies will get healthier and our stress levels will decrease (Proverbs 3:7-8; 4:20-23; 14:30).

Mental Effects

Destructive relationships make it extremely difficult to think calmly, clearly, and truthfully, especially when we feel frightened, intimidated, or deceived. Brad found that his problem-solving abilities deteriorated under the critical eye of his new boss. He made mistakes and missed crucial deadlines even though his previous work evaluations were always superior.

Rita (from chapter 1) never developed her ability to think for herself under the domineering eyes of her overprotective parents. Terri stopped thinking critically altogether. She deferred to John to keep peace, but that decision impacted her confidence in her abilities to manage her own life. She increasingly isolated herself, fearing that she was too stupid or too inept to offer her input in social situations such as at church or with her friends. She seemed genuinely surprised when anyone asked her opinion on things.

Confusion reigns when someone tells us one thing but our guts tell us another. Cindy began to think she was losing her mind when her husband Gary systematically lied to her about his relationship with his secretary. When we are habitually questioned or criticized or deceived, we begin to doubt our own judgment. We feel stupid or incompetent, and before long, like Brad, we often start acting that way as well.

Isolation is dangerous to our well-being. Sometimes a controlling partner purposely keeps us away from other relationships, but other times we intentionally separate ourselves from people because we feel inferior or ashamed, or because it's easier than interacting. Those in destructive relationships usually discover that when they engage with others—whether family members, work colleagues, friends, or even total strangers—their partner becomes jealous, angry, or punishing. Your partner may believe that he or she is entitled to your full and undivided attention. You may tell yourself that maintaining other relationships is not worth the price you have to pay. Don't believe it.

Even if isolating yourself works to keep peace in the short run, it becomes extremely unhealthy in the long run. As I have explained, we are impacted and affected by our relationships. If we only associate with destructive individuals, the total impact upon us is much greater than if we also have relationships with others who are loving, wise, and mature. Brad found comfort in his wife's words, which reminded him that he was a competent person and that his boss was emotionally abusive. The toxic effect of the destructive person upon us can be lessened when we invite and allow others to encourage us, pray for us, support us, and love us.

Relational Effects

Each one of the Ten Commandments focuses on some aspect of a relationship. The first four address how we are to relate with God. The next six address how we are to treat one another. When the apostle Paul sums up God's commandments, he concludes by saying,

> The commandments…and whatever other commands there
> may be, are summed up in this one rule: "Love your neighbor
> as yourself." Love does no harm to its neighbor. Therefore
> love is the fulfillment of the law (Romans 13:9-10 NIV).

God never minimizes the damage that sin causes to bodies, spirits, and minds, which is why he teaches us how to treat one another. Yet we are prone to underestimate the relational damage of sin, especially when it occurs between family members. We encourage people to forgive and be reconciled, which are good things to do, but how can we build a healthy relationship with someone we distrust, fear, or can't talk honestly or peaceably with? It's impossible.

Sin's destruction isn't merely personal, it's interpersonal. It rips apart relationships and sometimes irrevocably destroys them. Tamar was personally ruined by her half brother Amnon's selfishness, and their relationship was totally destroyed (2 Samuel 13:15). David's special friendship with King Saul ended when Saul became jealous of David and continually tried to harm him (1 Samuel 18–20). It took years for Esau to forgive his brother Jacob for deceiving their father and stealing his birthright (Genesis 27).

Perhaps one of the most serious long-term relational effects of interpersonal sin is how it shapes our view of ourselves and others. Because we are relational creatures, the effect can be profoundly damaging, especially to small children whose parents are emotionally, physically, or sexually abusive toward them. The best way to show how those who grow up in destructive environments see themselves in relationship to others is with a drawing.

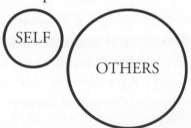

People who were abused or neglected as children by caretakers will likely see themselves as small, insignificant, unimportant, and needy. They may feel incapable, unworthy, or undeserving of anything good. When the most important people in their world don't value or honor them, victims become insecure and fearful. They don't see themselves in relationship with others as coequals. Most feel inferior to others, though on occasion they may defend themselves against painful feelings by inflating their own worth and acting as if they're superior.

From her earliest recollections, Sara's father told her that she was nothing but a whore. She tried everything to prove him wrong and win his approval, but when she was raped at 16 she concluded he must be right. She was no good. No decent man would be interested in her. After two failed marriages to destructive men, Sara tentatively began dating again. She told me she had met someone special, but after she got to know him better, she dumped him like a hot potato. "Why?" I asked her. "What was wrong with him?" She said, "Nothing. He was a good Christian man and came from a good family. He'd never be interested in me."

A NEED FOR COMPASSION AND WISDOM

Many people advised Brad to request a transfer out of his boss's department when they saw the toll it was taking on him. "She's a tyrant," they said. "No one can reason with her; she always has to be right." In contrast, Sally was encouraged by her Christian friends to "keep trying harder to be a good wife and hang in there," even though her husband treated her with continuous criticism and contempt.

I'm not suggesting that a marriage should be as easy to leave as a job is, or that men get more sympathy when mistreated than women do, but we all need to develop greater compassion and empathy for those trapped in destructive family relationships because the stakes are so high and the cost is so enormous. We also need greater wisdom to help these victims sort through the maze of their own sinful responses to what has been done to them. We need to know how to guide them in inviting their destructive partners to change. We will cover these topics more extensively in part 2.

Sara didn't end her new relationship because she had learned to identify destructive traits in potential partners and feared her new love interest was another destructive man. She ran from him because she was afraid he'd reject her once he got to know her better. She wasn't "good enough" for him. Deep down, she still saw herself as a whore, someone no decent person would want. Old lies don't easily die.

When you see yourself as small, others become larger than life. They are powerful, dangerous, strong, intimidating, wonderful, always right, definitely better than you, and always in control of the upper hand. When you view others in this way, you usually give them a lot of power over you. This is dangerous. If you feel inferior and defective like Sara does, you can't always make good choices about whom you allow yourself to get close to. When you give another person the power to define you, then you also give them the power to control you. Here's an example of how this works: You tell yourself that when someone you value loves you, that love proves you must be worth something. On the other hand, if they don't love you, you must be worthless—like a piece of garbage.

Many of Sara's difficulties with her current relationships stem from her upbringing. This leads us to look at the generational effects of destructive relationships, because sin's damage isn't only personal and interpersonal, it is intergenerational.

Generational Effects

Children suffer the effects of a destructive relationship even if they are only witnesses and not targets. If you engage in warfare in your home, whether with your spouse or a particular child or someone else living with you, please stop now. You will not want to pay the consequences of continuing. Recently I received an e-mail from a woman who learned this too late. She wrote, "Sometimes I wish I had learned earlier to flee evil. My children would not have the horrible memories that they are now working through."

The Bible warns us that the sins of the father are passed down from one generation to the next. (See Exodus 34, for example.) But what specifically does that look like?

Children learn how to see themselves, others, the world, and even God through their parents' eyes and actions. Children pick up on what makes life work and what's worth living for through the behaviors they witness at home, including destructive behaviors or attitudes not directed toward them. For example, many young boys living in homes where their fathers abuse their mothers learn that men have more power than women do. They observe that the way to get what they want is to threaten, force, or hit someone. They may even think that God entitles them to act this way because they're men, and that the Bible teaches that being the head of a home means they should always get to have their way.

When they're little boys, they may hate what's happening to their mothers, yet when they grow up and get married, they often repeat the same behaviors toward their own wives. How to think as men and how to act as husbands is passed down to them from their fathers. Many times these men marry women who also have grown up believing that women have no power or voice. Their mothers didn't, so why would they? And the destructive cycle continues to the next generation.

Not only is future behavior shaped by what we learn in childhood, our very genetic makeup is influenced by our home environments. Research in brain science shows some staggering findings that ought to make every parent pause. Goleman explains:

> The human brain is designed to change itself in response to accumulated experience…

> It had long been assumed that gene-controlling events were strictly biochemical—getting proper nutrition, or (in a worst case) exposure to industrial toxins. Now epigenetic studies are looking at how parents treat a growing child, finding ways child rearing shapes that child's brain…

> Like a plant adapting to rich or to depleted soil, a child's brain shapes itself to fit its social ecology, particularly the emotional climate fostered by the main people in her life.[7]

These studies demonstrate that our brain circuitry is hardwired over time by our repeated experiences and our closest relationships.

> Parenting cannot change every gene, nor modify every neural tic—and yet what children experience day after day sculpts their neural circuitry. Neuroscience has begun to pinpoint with surprising specificity how some of that sculpting operates.[8]

For those of us who may still have some faulty childhood wiring, the good news is that our brain can, to some extent, be rewired by regular involvement in loving and nurturing relationships. I believe that's one reason God commands us to learn to love well and to treat others with tenderhearted forgiveness and compassion. We have an opportunity to experience significant interpersonal healing through loving connection with others.

Growth, healing, and restoration are possible, no matter how much hurt we've experienced. To begin your own healing process, join a healthy body of believers and become a part of a small group where you can begin to experience new relationships. Your children's future is all the more reason to learn what healthy relationships are and to work hard to break destructive patterns.

Spiritual Effects

Any talk about the effects of destructive relationships would be incomplete without taking a look at the spiritual fallout. For most people in these kinds of relationships, God seems distant, unloving, and uninvolved. He appears small. During the psalmist's most difficult relationships, he repeatedly wanted to know why God didn't hear his prayers. (See Psalm 13, for example.) It's hard to believe God or trust him when he allows bad things to happen to us over and over again.

To other people, God feels like a cosmic cop, always looking to catch us and punish us for our wrongdoings. We know he's powerful, but we doubt his goodness and cannot feel his love.

Sin grieves God. It hurts his heart (Genesis 6:6). When people sin against him and against one another, God understands the devastating result. That's why he continually encourages us to learn to live righteously. My prayer is that as you work your way through the rest of this book, you will encounter God as he is truly is. Perhaps the best place to search for God is to look at Jesus. The Bible tells us that Christ perfectly represents the nature of God (Hebrews 1:3).

Jesus told stories to help us understand what God is like. He told us, for example, that God the Shepherd takes time to search for even one sheep that gets lost; it's that important to him (Matthew 18:12-14). In a different story, Jesus talked about a father who had two sons. One was rebellious and did terrible things. But when his wandering son returned broken and battered from the hardships of sinful living, his father welcomed him with open arms and even threw a party for him (Luke 15:11-32).

What is God like? Jesus showed us that no one is unimportant or disposable in God's eyes. He always had time to talk, even with only one person (as he did, for example, with the Samaritan woman of John 4). He made time to search for those who were lost and welcomed the foolish back without scorn or shame. Even now he celebrates our return and our repentance.

Jesus told us that God reaches out to us even when we don't make the first step, like the prodigal's father, who approached his other angry and bitter son (Luke 15). God doesn't only go to the broken and battered, but he also goes to the angry, the self-righteous, the judgmental, the jealous, and the proud. He loves them too!

Jesus shows us what God is like, and God is wonderful. He is full of grace and truth, mercy and love, and he wants to rescue you from the hand of the wicked, from the grasp of the cruel (Jeremiah 15:21).

3

What Makes Relationships Difficult and Destructive?

*All sin is based on original sin,
the effects of which will be with us till death.*

WILLIAM JOHNSTON

*Whoever stubbornly refuses to accept
criticism will suddenly be broken beyond repair.*

PROVERBS 29:1

⁓

W hen I was in college, I read a bestselling book by Thomas Harris called *I'm Okay, You're Okay*. It's a nice thought, but it just isn't true. Deep down I know I'm not okay, and I know you're not okay either. If I wrote a book and titled it *I'm Broken, and You're Broken Too,* it wouldn't sell very well—but it would be much closer to the truth.

Beautiful but Broken

God designed humankind magnificently. He wove his divine likeness into us and placed us just a little lower than angels (Psalm 8:5). When he finished, he said his creation was very good (Genesis 1:31). We have within us the capacity for incredible beauty and

63

goodness, but something went dreadfully wrong. We create breathtaking gardens, then trash our environment. We feed the homeless, then gossip about our neighbor's marital problems. We express kindness toward a stranger who asks us for directions, then yell at our kids or spouse because they bother us.

Why do our relationships fail? What damages them? What drives a person to injure another person's body, spirit, or soul and not even recognize those actions or attitudes as harmful?

As a licensed counselor, I could go into psychological explanations for some of the reasons people become destructive, but as a Christian counselor, I'd rather keep it simple: It's sin. But our sin isn't all that simple. Sin isn't only something people do wrong, sin is something we are, meaning we are fallen and broken beautiful people. Since Adam and Eve ate the forbidden fruit, humans don't function as well as God designed us to. Instead of asking God to teach us what is best, we lean toward going our own way, and we naturally prefer sin over righteousness. That's why we always need to be suspicious of what feels "normal." *Normal* is still *broken*.

We only have to look at a small child to know this is true. No one has to teach a toddler how to do wrong. That comes naturally (Psalm 51:5). When she doesn't get her way, she throws a temper tantrum. When she wants something her brother has, she hits him and grabs it away. As she gets older, when she's caught doing something she shouldn't do, she lies about what happened. The parents' job is to teach their children how to behave and how to recognize and admit their brokenness, which teaches humility, an important virtue that helps us maintain good relationships.[2]

Language is a funny thing. As a culture, we don't like to talk about *sin* and *evil* anymore. Good counselors definitely aren't supposed to use those words to describe the hurtful and horrible things people do to each other. Most of us don't even like to use the word *broken;* we prefer the words *wounded* and *sick*.

During a recent counseling session, I gently confronted my client Rachel about her temper and the harsh way she spoke to people. She told me, "It's because my mother never loved me. I'm hurt and I'm angry. I can't help it." My client was telling herself, *Because my mother hurt me, I'm wounded and I'm sick. Whenever I feel upset, the only thing I can do is to get so angry everyone knows they'd better not mess with me again. That's my mom's fault.*

Please don't misunderstand me. Rachel *is* wounded and sick and did suffer a great deal in her childhood due to her mother's neglectful and hurtful parenting.[3] She did not learn constructive ways to manage her feelings or her problems in life. As tragic as that is, her mother's behavior is not Rachel's main problem right now, nor is it the reason she acts the way she does. You see, if we are *only* wounded or sick, then we are not responsible. We can't help it; we're simply victims of what's been done to us.

We slide further into self-deception when we do what Adam and Eve did when God confronted them in the garden after they disobeyed him. Like the child who hits her brother because he wouldn't give her the toy she wanted, we blame the other person when we do wrong. We say, "They *made* us do it."

If they *made* us do it, then we're not sinful or broken—our condition is the other person's fault, we insist.

The Deadly Exchange

In the first chapter of Romans, the apostle Paul describes what went wrong in the garden as well as what's wrong with us today. He writes, "They traded the truth about God for a lie. So they worshiped and served the things God created instead of the Creator himself" (verse 25). Eve's decision to believe the serpent's lie put her desire for power and knowledge above God. Eve's desire wasn't the problem. She fell when she craved power and knowledge *more* than she loved God and his Word.

Eve's decision to believe the serpent's lie over what God told her forever changed her peaceful, loving way of life in the garden paradise that God provided. Satan promised Eve that if she believed him, she'd gain the ability to be like God. Instead, she lost her

innocence and discovered shame, hardship, and sorrow in her relationship with Adam.

When God confronted Adam and Eve for their disobedience,
Adam blamed Eve; Eve blamed the serpent, and the first destructive
relationship pattern was set into motion. It took only one generation for the result of those seemingly harmless choices to grow
deadly. Cain, Adam and Eve's first child, envied and murdered his
younger brother Abel and felt no remorse (Genesis 4:9).

Paul continues to explain the consequences of this deadly
exchange:

> Their lives became full of every kind of wickedness, sin,
> greed, hate, envy, murder, quarreling, deception, mali-
> cious behavior, and gossip. They are backstabbers, haters of
> God, insolent, proud, and boastful. They invent new ways
> of sinning, and they disobey their parents. They refuse to
> understand, break their promises, are heartless, and have
> no mercy (Romans 1:29-31).

Relational destructiveness is the indirect consequence of our
inborn tendency to reject God as God and truth as truth, Paul says.
His teaching is critical if we are to understand some of what happens
in destructive relationship patterns. He says that our problems are
caused by things *we do,* not only by things that are *done to us.*

This concept is difficult to grab hold of, because it's hard to see our
part of the problem when it's obvious that another person's behavior
is destroying us. Without a doubt, my mother's words and actions
caused harm to me as a young child. Even as an adult, she had the
power to devastate me with her tongue—until I stopped letting her.
As long as I believed her words were more true than God's Word, she
had the power to destroy me—because I gave it to her.

During one incident in my late twenties, I remember her telling
me that she hated me and wished I was dead. After I angrily
responded with a few choice words of my own, I stumbled out
of her house feeling like I wanted to die. I distinctly remember

hearing God say to my heart, *Leslie, she is broken. She will never love you like you want her to, but I love you and you are special to me.* I chose to believe him. From that day on, my mother's words lost their power over me. It wasn't that they never hurt, but they never destroyed me again. My internal healing didn't mean I instantly gained the ability to respond to her cruelty with wisdom and grace. That maturity took much longer to develop.

When the Pharisees rejected Jesus and told people he was either crazy or from Satan (Matthew 12:24), Jesus felt the deep pain of rejection, but he was not destroyed by it. Why not? Because Jesus knew what was true, and he knew who he was. We're not Jesus and are therefore vulnerable to believing lies over truth, just like Paul warns us.

Jesus also cautions us that Satan is a deceiver (John 8:44). His mission is to kill, steal, and destroy (John 10:10). Throughout the Gospels, Jesus proclaims again and again that he is giving us God's truth. Not only that, Jesus claims he *is* God's truth (John 14:6). When we know him and believe him, we gain wisdom and strength to navigate the difficult waters of messy relationships. He equips us to recognize lies and learn how to reject them. We will learn how to do this more in parts 2 and 3.

Even as Christians, we struggle with unbelief. We embrace the truth of the gospel and the Bible, yet when we're honest, many of us have a hard time actually trusting God with our daily lives. The effect of our brokenness is that we have become separated from God, from others, and from ourselves. We have a divided mind, conflicting emotions, a natural orientation toward self, and a will that is more willing to please ourselves or please others than to please God. Lies we believe can destroy us, and what we love the most will control us. That's why God tells us to believe him and to not love anything more than we love him.

What We Worship (Love) Controls Us

Roy said, "I'm not into worship, Leslie," as we were talking about his faith. What he really meant was that he didn't like going to church or singing hymns or praise choruses. But he was most definitely into worship—worship of success, achievement, and financial security. Everything Roy did served those three gods. One of the reasons he was in counseling was because his marriage was in shambles due to his long work hours and neglect of his family. Roy rationalized that he was just trying to be a good provider, but truth be told, he loved the praise, admiration, and recognition he received from his achievements and success far more than he loved his wife and children. Jesus warns us that where our treasure is, there our hearts will be also (Matthew 6:21).

God made all people to be worshippers. Our need to worship is part of our DNA like an internal compass that always points toward true north. However, when people choose not to worship God, it doesn't mean they don't worship at all. We all worship something (or someone) that we value, love, or are deeply impressed with.

As Americans, we kneel down to the gods of productivity, achievement, and efficiency, power and control, beauty and youth, approval and acceptance, success and status, sex and food. Many women I know are controlled by the words of the mirror and scale every morning and have a good or bad day depending on what they say. God knows our tendencies toward idolatry (loving false gods). That's why the first four of the Ten Commandments specifically have to do with our relationship with him. He knows how essential it is to our emotional, physical, relational, and spiritual health that we honor, love, and value him above all else.

Satan always appeals to our human desires and felt needs and continually offers us god substitutes to distract us from our true longing and deep need for God. God warns us not to put any other gods before him (see Deuteronomy 5 and 6) because he knows that if we do, we will be captured or destroyed by them.

The book of Ezekiel illustrates this in Israel's history. The biggest sin Israel committed was spiritual adultery (Ezekiel 16:32). Her heart grew cold as she turned from loving and depending on God for her well-being and happiness to created things. Israel embraced the lie that God wasn't enough and that following God kept her from the good life. She believed the same core lie that Satan fed Eve in the garden. Like Eve and Israel, we too would rather decide for ourselves what we think is good, true, and right instead of believing, trusting, and obeying God.

We all wrestle with disorders of worship and believing lies even if we're not in a destructive relationship. That is why we're still broken. For many of us, lies feel truer than the truth does. It's easier to believe that God hates us or is angry with us than it is to believe that we are his beloved children and are precious to him. We meditate again and again on some hurtful words someone has said, yet when another person pays us a compliment, we dismiss it or don't trust it, even if that person is genuine.

WHERE IS *LIFE* FOUND?

Jesus urges us to stay away from false gods and reminds us that *life* is found in God and not in the things (even good things) God gives us. Jesus commands us to love God with all of our hearts, minds, souls, and strength, because he knows that this love relationship is the only love relationship that will completely satisfy us. In his wonderful book *The Evidential Power of Beauty*, spiritual director Thomas Dubay writes,

> You and I, each and every one of us without exception, can be defined as an aching need for the infinite. Some people realize this; some do not. But even the latter illustrate this inner ache when, not having God deeply, they incessantly spill themselves out into excitements and experiences, licit or illicit. They are trying to fill their inner emptiness, but they never succeed, which is why the search is incessant. Though worldly pleasure seeking never fulfills and satisfies in a continuing way, it may tend momentarily to distract and to dull the profound pain of the inner voice. If these people allow themselves a moment of reflective silence (which they seldom do), they notice a still, small voice whispering, *Is this all there is?* They begin to sense a thirst to love with abandon, without limit, without end, without lingering aftertastes of bitterness...
>
> How they and we respond to this inner outreach rooted in our deep spiritual soul is the most basic set of decisions we can make; they have eternal consequences.[4]

If you're in a destructive relationship, you can't change the other person or control what he or she does or says. But if you want to break free, you must recognize that you have given this person God's authority over your life and allowed his or her words to become *truth* and the *words of life and death* to you. Parts 2 and 3 will help you learn how to reverse this tendency as well as give you specific tools to address destructiveness in your relationships.

It's true that our brokenness (*dysfunction* is the secular term), causes much pain and heartache and can make our relationships difficult. The even deeper problem is what we do with our brokenness. That decision determines whether we grow healthier and more like Christ in spite of our brokenness, or become destructive toward others as well as toward ourselves.

Our Response to Our Brokenness

Jesus saves people from the penalty of sin. He also redeems us from the power of sin (Romans 8:2; 2 Peter 1:3). This reality is the good news of the gospel. One of the definitions of the biblical Greek word for salvation (*sozo*) is the idea of restoration, wholeness, or healthiness.[5] God's salvation is not merely forgiveness of sin so that we get to heaven someday, but a blueprint that includes our maturity and restoration. Becoming emotionally whole and spiritually holy is the journey God desires for each of us as we work out our salvation within the context of our relationships.

Let's take a look at how God teaches us to respond to our brokenness. As we mature emotionally and spiritually, this pattern becomes a part of our character so that our brokenness doesn't lead to destructiveness. As you read this, ask yourself if you practice any of these steps in your own interactions with others. If not (which may be the case), you can begin to grow by adopting new behaviors. Perhaps you've never been in a relationship where you saw these modeled. God's plan for you is to become whole and holy. You may not be able to get others to do these things, but don't let that stop you from growing and becoming healthier.

Healthy (Mature) Responses to Brokenness

1. Learn how to see. James tells us that "we all stumble in many ways" (James 3:2 NIV), but if we don't see where we stumble, we can't avoid falling. That might sound obvious, but many people cannot or will not see their brokenness or sin. For example, Jesus called the Pharisees "blind" because they denied their pride and self-righteousness (John 9:35-41). You can't work on a problem or ask for help if you won't see or can't acknowledge the problem exists. The psalmist prayed that God would show him his hidden faults (Psalm 139:24).

Most of the time, our awareness comes when we see we have hurt someone, or they tell us that we've done something that pains them. When I yanked Ryan to his feet that day and dislocated his elbow, I immediately recognized my behavior as abusive. I knew abuse because I had been abused. I did not want to be the kind of mother who abused her children, yet I knew that I had that tendency. I saw it. It was part of my sinful brokenness. On the other hand, my mother was never able to see or admit her brokenness until the later stages of her life. For many years she could not acknowledge her drinking problem or that she ever treated her children wrongly.

2. Face your brokenness and ask for forgiveness. Helen came to see me after her husband, Richard, moved out of the house. He said that he couldn't live with her temper and disrespect any longer. She yelled and criticized him constantly, and when he told her it upset him, she called him a baby and mocked him. He finally concluded he wasn't important to her—her words and actions said it loud and clear.

Helen knew Richard was upset—he said these things lots of times before—but she had never taken his words to heart. She rationalized that he was oversensitive and didn't understand how much stress she was under or how busy she was with the kids.

Helen didn't want to look at herself to find the reasons for her behavior. Instead, she made excuses and started pointing out all her husband's faults.

But Helen began to realize that if she wanted any hope of winning her husband back, she needed to become more aware of the way she treated him and also had to admit she had a problem. She began to acknowledge that her disrespectful yelling and screaming were wrong and not a healthy way to communicate, even when her husband aggravated her. Eventually she wrote him a letter saying she understood why he left her and told him he was right—he shouldn't tolerate that kind of behavior from her. She asked him to forgive her. The next step for Helen was to think about what she could do to change her destructive behavior.

To become more aware of the true nature of our actions, it is important to consider the feedback significant others give us regarding our behaviors or attitudes. For example, if Tom's pastor (chapter 1) had listened to Tom's concerns, confessed his dishonesty, and asked Tom's forgiveness, they could have ended their ministry relationship on better terms. Ideally Tom's pastor should have asked himself why he wasn't honest in the first place and tried to discern what was underneath his dishonesty. Was it jealousy of Tom's ministry success? Was it fear of disapproval or conflict? Answering these questions would have increased the pastor's growth and had a healing effect upon their relationship.

Pride often keeps us from seeing or admitting our brokenness to others. Don't let your pride blind you.

3. *Take responsibility for your part of the problem.* Helen wasn't responsible for every problem in her marriage, but she needed to take responsibility for her part. That's why Jesus tells us to take the plank out of our own eye before we attempt to remove the speck from someone else's eye (Matthew 7:3).

At first, Helen was tempted to tell herself that she couldn't change. Her mother treated her father far worse than she treated Richard, and at least she was doing better than her mother did. But Helen knew that God didn't want her to be disrespectful and harsh toward her husband, even when she was angry or disappointed with him. She began to feel sorry for hurting him, and she wanted to learn how to be different. She was willing to do the work to get there.

When I recognized my abusive tendencies toward my son, I needed to take responsibility for my anger and actions regardless of my upbringing or Ryan's misbehavior. Certainly those factors influenced me, but I could not control or change them. The only thing I could change was my response.

Admitting our own wrongdoing apart from all other factors, and working on responding differently even when someone else is clearly in the wrong, is part of becoming emotionally and spiritually mature.

4. *Make the effort to change.* *Repentance* means much more than feeling guilt or shame or even being sorry over wrong behaviors and hurtful attitudes. With God's help, we must turn from them and do the work to be different. Paul tells us that we're to put off our old selves and put on our new selves, which he tells us is created to resemble God's likeness (Ephesians 4:20–5:1).

Helen stayed in counseling in order to learn how to handle her negative moods in a godly way and how to be more sensitive to her spouse's needs and feelings. When she slipped and blurted out nasty words, or when Richard told Helen she was being disrespectful to him, now she paid attention. She stopped making excuses for herself and walked herself through the first three steps of this process again...and again...and again...until they became a part of who she was (and wanted to be).

Whenever Helen became discouraged, she reminded herself that God was not finished with his work in her heart. He promised to change her, and Helen committed herself to cooperate with him to that end, however long it took.

Remember, because we are all sinful, some pain in relationships is unavoidable. However, when two people are mature enough to respond to each other using the steps outlined above, their relationship does not become destructive. I'm saddened by the truth that people often make the opposite choice.

Immature (Unhealthy) Responses to Brokenness

Most of us do not readily recognize our own sinfulness. It's hard to look in the mirror and detect what's really in our hearts. Our nature is to lie to ourselves about ourselves (Jeremiah 17:9). God already knows that is humankind's tendency. That's one of the reasons he mandates community and connection. Within our relationships, we are to stimulate one another toward greater maturity (see Ephesians 4), to admonish each other when necessary (1 Thessalonians 5:14), and encourage one another to live in truth, because any one of us can become self-deceived (Hebrews 3:13).

However, when we are told what we are doing is wrong, or if we see we are hurting a person, many of us close our ears, refuse to hear the truth, become defensive, rationalize, blame others, make excuses, or lie about our actions.

Refusal to listen, defensiveness. During a counseling session with me, Bob's wife tried to talk with him about his inappropriate behavior toward her. He actually put his fingers in his ears and sang, "La la la la la la..." He did not want to hear about or acknowledge his destructiveness, and he resorted to childish ways to remain unaware.

Sue came to me because she could not understand why conversations with her husband, Mark, always ended with her feeling like she did something wrong. Sue shared that she recently told Mark she wanted to talk with him about some things that were troubling her. He bristled and didn't seem receptive. So later on she said to him, "Hon, lately it seems like we're walking on eggshells around here. Is something wrong?" Mark didn't respond. So Sue added, "I'm concerned about something I observed with the kids. Saturday you promised to take them to the park, but you never did. That's not the first time. I'm worried that the kids are getting hurt and will lose confidence in you."

She didn't tell Mark that earlier in the day she had overheard her older son whisper to the younger one, "Don't count on it," when their dad promised to take them to the pool. Even so, when Sue shared her concerns, Mark erupted and yelled at her. "I know I'm a lousy dad. I don't know why I even bother trying. I will never be good enough for you, will I?"

Sue felt devastated and tried to clarify her intent. She said, "I'm not trying to hurt you. I just want to have a normal conversation with you. I don't think you're a horrible father, but I do want to share some things that might help you be a better dad to our boys." Mark would have no part of it. He stormed out of the house, leaving Sue believing she had done something terribly wrong. This type of conversation wasn't unusual; it was their typical pattern of interaction.

Mark's guard was always up. Sue found it challenging to share her feelings about what he did or how he impacted their boys without Mark falling into self-pity or self-hatred. Sue longed for a relationship with her husband where honest feedback could be shared. She couldn't control Mark or his responses, but Mark definitely controlled her. By regularly twisting what Sue said and accusing her of attacking him, he effectively stopped all healthy conversation and constructive feedback Sue could give him. By the time Mark was done with Sue, she felt like Mark was right: she was a horrible wife.

People like Mark are not willing to listen to others, and talking with them goes nowhere. The normal give-and-take of effective communication and healthy interaction feels impossible. An extremely unhealthy response to seeing our brokenness and sin is to become self-destructive. Judas became so distraught after recognizing what he had done to Jesus that he went out and hanged himself (Matthew 27:1-10).

The maturing person allows others to act as mirrors that reflect the truth of his or her life. That doesn't mean that everything everyone says about us is always true, it just means that when someone shares a concern about the way we are behaving toward others, we ought to at least check it out. The Bible tells us that "as iron sharpens iron, so a friend sharpens a friend" (Proverbs 27:17).

Blindness and denial. Jesus says that the person who consistently rejects constructive feedback from others is blind as well as foolish. *Denial,* the psychological term, is a defense against seeing one's brokenness. People on the defense cannot see themselves truthfully, nor can they own the pain and suffering they cause others. They cannot acknowledge that they are doing anything wrong, hurtful, sinful, or inappropriate. They have an answer for everything that makes perfect sense according to their own version of reality, even if it leaves you scratching your head or thinking you're going crazy.

Even when Jesus rebuked the Pharisees and called them a brood of vipers (Matthew 23:32), they still refused to see their own proud hearts. Here is Christ's description of destructive blindness:

> Your eye is a lamp that provides light for your body. When your eye is good, your whole body is filled with light. But when your eye is bad, your whole body is filled with darkness. And if the light you think you have is actually darkness, how deep that darkness is! (Matthew 6:22–23).

Remember, the self-deceived person who believes that he or she sees clearly can be most dangerous. Jim Jones, a self-proclaimed religious prophet and leader for the Peoples Temple, confidently led over 600 adults to commit mass suicide in 1978 in Jonestown,

Guyana, by drinking cyanide-laced grape juice and giving it to their children. Over 900 people died.

In his day, Jesus warned people about the destructiveness of the Pharisees when he told them to guard against their teaching (Matthew 16:6,12). God never intended for us to be able to discern all truth all by ourselves. That's why he has provided us with his Word and one another as a protection against our tendency toward deception.

Unwillingness to change. In addition to blindness or denial, another common deadly pattern of responding to our brokenness is the flippant *I know, I'm sorry* response. In other words, a person is aware of the sin and acknowledges that he or she has a problem, feels sorry, but then does nothing to change. We will learn more about how to evaluate this pattern biblically when we get to chapters 8 and 9, where you will learn whether to keep persevering in a difficult relationship or to step back from a destructive person who will not change.

Be careful. Because we are all broken, most of us will question our own thinking or perceptions at times. This is usually a good thing. But we should also feel free to question other people's thinking. Don't believe everything everyone tells you. Check out the claims for yourself against God's Word. Seek wisdom from people who know you and respect you. When I began to believe other people really saw me differently than my own mother did, I experienced a new level of healing. They liked me and even enjoyed me. I wasn't perfect but I was loved, and that felt pretty good.

Our Response to One Another's Brokenness

Just as it can be painful to *see* our own brokenness, it can also be difficult to recognize the brokenness of the people who share our destructive relationships, especially when we love them and can see their good qualities. Like we do in our own lives, we make excuses for them, cover for them, lie for them, or protect them from the painful consequences of their own actions.

We continue to try to please them, appease them, or change them, but no matter how hard we try, the damage continues. Or we may sit as judge and jury over them, forgetting that we too are broken.

In parts 2 and 3, I will provide some specific steps you can take to build greater spiritual and emotional health into your life so that you can respond rightly to the sins of others. Closing our eyes and pretending nothing is happening isn't the answer. Neither is harshness, judgment, and criticism, or trying to change them into the people we think they should be.

Healthy, mature people allow reality and truth to teach them. Unhealthy individuals blame life or others instead of learning the laws of God's world; for example, you can't put your hand on a hot stove and not get burned. Healthy, mature people look to God's truth to shape their ideas. (See Psalm 119, especially verse 29, for the psalmist's commitment to this process.) Destructive people twist or distort God's Word to prove they are right or get their own way.

When you are in relationship with those who refuse to see their own brokenness or admit their blindness, you are in great danger. Be careful not to allow another's blindness to become your blindness. Remember, we are highly influenced by other people. The more dependent we are on others for our physical and emotional safety and well-being, the more susceptible and suggestible we become. In extreme cases, some individuals develop a disorder called Stockholm syndrome, whereby the victim no longer views the abuser as the enemy. Instead, the victim becomes emotionally bonded with the abuser. This syndrome has been documented in kidnap victims and concentration camp survivors; it has also been observed in battered spouses and abused children.

To understand more clearly the roots of destructive behaviors, we must now look more closely at what is going on within the hearts of those who are blind and destructive.

4

Destructive Themes of the Heart: Pride, Anger, and Envy

*It seems easier to be God than to love God,
easier to control people than to love people.*

HENRI NOUWEN

*You look deep within the mind and heart,
O righteous God.*

PSALM 7:9

B rian and Sandra began arguing in my office. "It's your fault," Brian said. "I can never tell you the real truth because every time I try, you explode with outrageous accusations and won't let me explain. You've accused me of hiding the truth from you since the day we got married."

"That's so untrue," Sandra retorted. "The reason I explode is that you give me no choice. When you lie to me with the small stuff, how can I possibly trust you with the big things?"

As the argument escalated, I broke into their blame game with a simple illustration. I reached over to my shelf and grabbed a glass jar filled with water. A small amount of sediment they could not see had settled to the bottom. I vigorously shook the jar, and the water began to turn a muddy brown. I turned to Brian and Sandra and asked, "Did shaking the jar make the water dirty?" (I love easy questions.) Obviously the answer was no. Shaking the jar didn't dirty the water. Shaking the jar exposed the dirt that had settled along the bottom.

Sandra's explosive temper may push Brian's buttons, but her anger does not make Brian lie to Sandra. Brian's deception contributes to Sandra's mistrust of him, but his lies do not cause her explosive temper or suspicious nature.

EXAMINING OURSELVES

Why people do what they do is a question that has plagued philosophers, psychologists, moralists, and religious leaders for centuries. The underlying reasons behind habitual destructive behavior can be identified by examining what's going on inside of us. The Bible calls it the *heart*. This inward inspection is important for several reasons.

1. As I've explained, *we're often blind to what's happening in our own hearts*. It's easier to see the sins of another person than to look at our own faults. It's true that Brian and Sandra provoke one another, but their responses to provocation expose the inner workings of their hearts. Since the only hearts we can take responsibility for changing are our own, it is essential in our own healing that, as much as possible, we remove any blind spots in our lives and relationships.

2. If you are a people helper and don't understand the underlying heart issues at work in someone's problems, *you may unintentionally cause more harm than genuine growth*. For example, if people are controlling and abusive toward others because they want their own way and aren't getting it, merely focusing on their sinful behaviors without exposing the deeper heart themes of selfishness and pride may only teach them how to use more socially acceptable strategies to get their own way.

3. If you are in a destructive relationship (or are helping someone

else through one) and your partner indicates a desire to change destructive patterns, *it's important that you know what genuine change looks like at the heart level.* Awareness of destructive heart themes will increase your awareness of the fruits of genuine repentance.

4. *Recognizing destructive patterns as well as the heart themes that fuel those patterns will help you when seeking healthier relationships.* It is crucial that you learn what to look for so you don't continue to step into the same relationship problems again and again.

Our Hearts Exposed

Jesus tells us something very important that sheds light on why we do what we do (and why others do what they do). He says,

> A good person produces good things from the treasury of a good heart, and an evil person produces evil things from the treasury of an evil heart. What you say flows from what is in your heart (Luke 6:45-46).

Contrary to Hollywood or Harlequin, the human heart contains more than mere passion. Biblically, the term *heart* is much broader. It encompasses our feelings, as well as our thoughts and our beliefs, our values, deepest desires, motivations, and decisions.[1] It functions as an internal lens by which we see life and make decisions about what to do. Our hearts' desires stimulate us as well as motivate us toward action, whether godly or sinful. Asking ourselves the question, "What do I want, crave, need, hope for, or passionately desire?" is a quick way to peer into what is going on in our hearts.

Brian wanted time to explain himself and win Sandra's trust. Sandra wanted Brian's total honesty, even with little details. What's tricky in this case is what Sandra and Brian desired from each other wasn't bad or wrong. Trust and honesty are good things, yet Brian and Sandra wanted these badly enough to justify sinning against each other when they didn't get what they wanted.

When we become Christians, God gives us new hearts with the capacity for new thoughts, new beliefs, new values, new desires, and new motivations, as well as different feelings (Romans 6). We need to feed and nurture these new hearts and guard them against lies (told by ourselves or by others), because everything we do flows from either our old hearts (the Bible calls it our old nature) or our new hearts.

Stirring Up Issues

Think about this: As you reflect upon your interactions with people, how do you usually respond when you're upset or when someone is disappointed with you? Jesus points out that the way we interact with other people gives us a snapshot of our hearts. Do your actions reveal a loving heart that is eager to forgive and reconcile when there is a problem? Or is your heart more often fearful and anxious, always trying to say the right thing or not make anyone angry? Perhaps you notice that your words and actions reveal your heart is demanding, critical, impatient, or selfish with others.

The purpose of self-examination isn't to shame us or make us hate ourselves. Quite the contrary: God wants to help us face our problems before they get worse. Just like a mirror helps us see that a tiny sore on our nose may need a biopsy, or our bathroom scale tells us the hard truth that we've gained more than a few pounds, these glimpses that expose our hearts are meant to help us see the truth about ourselves or our partner. That is a good thing, because we can't stop something we can't see or change something we won't acknowledge.

As we've already learned, we are often blind to the true condition of our own hearts. Instead of seeing what we do as hurtful or sinful, our human tendency is to rationalize or blame the other person in the relationship for the way we react. Like Brian and Sandra, we say, "If only you wouldn't have done that, then I wouldn't have acted that way," or, "It's your fault I lost my temper, you should have _____." (You can fill in the blank.)

But when we make excuses, we're not thinking truthfully. We're telling ourselves that somehow the other person made us behave in a certain way. At first glance, it might seem true; after all, people provoke us all the time. But what happens in our hearts when we are provoked or agitated is the key to the real truth (even when the other person's behaviors are clearly wrong).

If I had started with totally clean water, I could have shaken that jar until my arm fell off and would have ended up with clean water. The water *looked* clean to Brian and Sandra, but shaking the jar exposed the truth. The water wasn't as clean as it appeared.

In the same way, when we are in difficult relationships, dirty issues get stirred up in our own hearts. This truth is healing because—and I'll keep saying this—the only heart you can work on is your own. Although you can be a powerful influence upon another person, you cannot change another person's heart. That is something only the other person and God can do.

Observing and Investigating

As we learned in chapter 3, the first step toward emotional and spiritual wholeness is to start becoming more aware of our heart issues by listening to feedback and observing ourselves more honestly. Listen to your words (both the words you say out loud as well as the ones that remain in your thoughts). Notice your feelings, your desires, and how you interact with people. As we practice paying attention, we get a good picture of what is going on in our own hearts even during seemingly insignificant events.

For example, when I find myself always feeling impatient with people, family and strangers alike, what's going on in my heart? I can blame my children for not doing what they were told or the poky driver in front of me for holding me up. But truth be told, those things aren't the *cause* of my impatience, they're merely the trigger that exposes it. Let's dig deeper. We already know I'm feeling impatient, but why? What am I telling myself?

Here is a peek into my internal self-talk. *Why can't my children just do what they are told for a change? Why do I have to say everything three or four times to be heard? It's not fair.* Or, *Why is this person driving so slow? Don't they notice they're holding up everyone else? I'm so frustrated. I can't stand it.* Another way to peek into what's going on in my heart is to ask myself what I want. *I want my way! I want life to go easy! I don't want people to get in my way. I don't want to be bothered or made to wait.* Now perhaps we're getting a clearer picture of where my impatience is coming from. My heart is thinking only of myself. My heart is self-centered and selfish at the moment. *My* wants, *my* needs, and *my* desires are preeminent, and I am mildly angry about not getting what I want. My external impatience is simply a reflection of this internal reality.

If I don't investigate the root of my impatience and merely focus on learning to not express impatience outwardly, my impatience will never be conquered, even if I gain reasonable self-control over its expression. I cannot overcome my impatience if I never address the internal heart themes of entitlement and self-centeredness. This concept is crucial when working toward changing a destructive relationship. Whether you are the victim of a destructive person or you are helping someone else through it, do not merely take behavioral changes as evidence of repentance. We are looking for a change of heart.

Jesus reminds us that our relationship difficulties start internally, not externally. For example, the Bible commands us not to murder others, but Jesus also insists that we root out the deeper attitudes that cause us to hate others or to feel angry with them. (See the Sermon on the Mount, Matthew 5–7.) Christ further clarifies our internal heart problems when he says,

"Don't you understand yet?" Jesus asked. "Anything you eat passes through the stomach and then goes into the sewer. But the words you speak come from the heart—that's what defiles you. For from the heart come evil thoughts, murder, adultery, all sexual immorality, theft, lying, and slander" (Matthew 15:16-19).

Unless we allow God to show us our unhealthy ways of responding to our brokenness, and until we are willing to change, our destructive relationships will not get better. Understanding ourselves doesn't simply mean getting in touch with our feelings. It also involves becoming aware of the thoughts behind the feelings and recognizing the lies we tell ourselves that feel so true. A man with serious control issues may feel enraged when his wife disagrees with him, and he may be adept at owning and expressing his anger. However, he may remain quite blind to the lies of entitlement that fuel that anger, or to the internal beliefs that justify and rationalize his cruel outbursts.

Knowing ourselves means we examine our hearts to discover what rules us and what we live for. When we see repetitive patterns that are hurtful toward others, we must do more than just name our sinful behaviors. Christ calls us to be ruled by his love and to live for his purposes. We cannot do this without a clear view of our brokenness.

Patterns of the Heart

When we're in the midst of destructive relationships with others, understanding their destructive heart themes is as important as identifying ours. Though we aren't responsible for changing anyone's heart but our own, perceiving the truth of what's happening will help us take appropriate action. Sometimes what's going on in another person is not so clear or easy to see. That's why outside counsel may be necessary and beneficial.

Discerning the deeper heart themes in others' lives is not an exercise in judging them. We are not better than they are. We are all broken. However, we do not want to be fooled into thinking someone is one way when he or she is another. What looks good on the surface may still be rotten underneath. Remember, Judas betrayed Jesus with a kiss. We want to be wise so that we are able to discern if repentance is from the heart or merely outward conformity. Since God's Word calls us all to truth seeking and truth telling, we need to understand some of the ways a person's heart (thoughts, feelings, desires, beliefs, values, and choices) develops an interpersonal style that injures others and wrecks relationships.

It is impossible to be spiritually mature when we are emotionally unhealthy. As Christians, we will continue to struggle with some of the habits of our old nature even as we grow, because they are still a real part of our brokenness. (See Ephesians 4 or Colossians 3 for Paul's teaching on this.) But as we strengthen our new nature, our new, healthier self won't want to be influenced or controlled by our old nature anymore. (See Paul's struggle in Romans 7, and read Galatians 5 for his teaching.) We may still have thoughts and feelings we don't like, even sinful or destructive ones, but they no longer have us. We are not ruled by them, nor are we blind to them. This distinction is a crucial part of becoming emotionally and spiritual healthy and whole.

As we begin to look at how the Bible describes the inner workings of our hearts, it's worth mentioning that every person's heart will contain some of these elements some of the time. No one is without sin for very long in his or her heart (1 John 1:8). However, what we are looking for are dominant life themes that repeat themselves over and over again in relationships.

As mentioned in chapter 3, the biggest problem in destructive relationships is not merely sin. Jesus is more than sufficient to handle our sins, even big ones. Our bigger problem is denial or blindness, inability or refusal to see or take personal responsibility for our habitual or repetitive sins. The biblical term is *hardness of heart*. Remember, Jesus strongly rebuked the Pharisees because they would not see their own sin. As a result they misled and hurt others ❦ and ultimately destroyed themselves (Matthew 23:5-36).

In the rest of this chapter as well as in chapter 5, we will examine seven specific internal heart patterns: the proud heart, the angry heart, the envious heart, the selfish heart, the lazy heart, the evil heart, and the fearful heart. As we examine these heart patterns individually, please note that these sins usually work together and feed off one another, causing great cumulative harm to individuals, churches, and families.

The Proud Heart

> Pride goes before destruction.
> PROVERBS 16:18

Not all pride is bad. It isn't sinful to feel good about our accomplishments or to enjoy the gifts that God has put within us as we use them to glorify him. The pride that God hates is an attitude that says, *I don't need God or his guidelines in my life. I want to call all the shots myself.* A proud heart will not bow to God as Lord. Instead of surrendering to God, the proud heart functions as its own god. The proud person wants to be his own authority and have his own power. A proud person centers his life not on God but on himself. Because our wills and our desires always revolve around what we want the most, the proud person is self-centered and self-focused.

A proud heart may suffer from an inferiority complex or low self-esteem, even though these problems may seem incompatible with a heart ruled by pride. However, the insecure yet proud don't feel inferior due to moral failures or spiritual inadequacies, but rather because they don't measure up to the things they crave or believe are essential for their well-being. Professor and psychologist Solomon Schimmel says this in his book *The Seven Deadly Sins:*

They don't typically ruminate about how unkind, dishonest, or insensitive they might be, but about how incompetent, ugly, or professionally unsuccessful they are. They do not aspire to greater virtue but to greater recognition.[2]

The proud will not be held accountable for their actions, nor will they answer to anyone. They may be quite religious and know Scripture backward and forward, but they use God to serve their personal agenda. They twist Bible passages to support their positions, to prove they're right, or to get what they want. When another person's perspective or beliefs are presented, they refuse to listen. Why would they need to? They're always right.

Pride and Blindness

Biblically, many of the Pharisees typified the destructive proud heart. Jesus found it impossible to have a productive conversation with them. Don't beat yourself up if you don't succeed in having a constructive or meaningful conversation with a proud person either. There is no use in disagreeing or presenting another point of view, because a proud heart will not acknowledge that there is another legitimate way of seeing things. Reality and truth is determined by what the proud person believes or says, not necessarily by what is factual or biblical. (See John 9 for a good example of the Pharisees' attempt to rewrite reality to suit their blind perspective.)

Debbie's pastor referred her to me. He told me she was rebellious and disrespectful toward her husband, and he was concerned that their marriage was in deep trouble. Debbie was beautiful, intelligent, and knew her Bible well. She deeply desired to honor God in her marriage but readily acknowledged that she was broken. After years of being humiliated and demeaned by her husband, she found herself responding back to him with criticism and contempt. She used her quick wit and sharp tongue as weapons to strike back because she felt abused, ignored, and dismissed.

Debbie and I worked together for over a year to change her

destructive attitude and responses toward her husband before I invited him to come to counseling with her. Debbie was not blind to her sin, and she could work on herself, but Debbie could not fix her marriage on her own. When I asked her husband to share what he thought he needed to change to make their marriage better, he could not think of a single thing. He could not think of any way in which he might have hurt Debbie. I asked John about the long lectures; Debbie had told me she and the kids were forced to sit through hours and hours of ranting and raving whenever they disagreed with him. I asked about his demands for absolute and unquestioning obedience to his authority.

John didn't flinch over his outrageous actions. From his perspective, Debbie should be a loving, submissive wife, which to him meant she should not question his judgment or decisions. If she questioned or argued with him, from his perspective, he had every right to lecture and discipline her. John could not see at all that his behavior hurt his family. Why not? Because his pride blinded him, and the teaching he received at church, I'm sad to say, contributed to that blindness (Psalm 36:2).

Tyrants and Narcissists

Those with proud hearts won't admit they are broken. They can't say, "I was wrong," or "I don't know how," or "I need help." If they ever say, "I'm sorry," the apology is always followed by "*but you...*" The most injurious thing about pride is that it thoroughly blinds people to their own proud hearts and any of their other sins, yet they have 20/20 vision for the faults and weaknesses of others.

> *Some people curse their father and do not thank their mother.*
> *They are pure in their own eyes, but they are filthy and unwashed.*
> *They look proudly around, casting disdainful glances.*
> *They have teeth like swords and fangs like knives.*
>
> —PROVERBS 30:11-14

Be careful around people who have proud hearts. They can be quite charming and make you feel as if you are at the center of their world. Don't be fooled. You are placed in the center of that world for one reason: to meet their felt needs. We can tell this because their thoughts, feelings, beliefs, ways of doing things, perspectives, and needs *always* come first, and people in their lives are objects, not companions who have their own feelings, needs, desires, and wants. The proud expect you to do what they say, their way, all the time. If you fail or refuse, the proud will punish you or resort to threats or force in order to gain power and control over you.

Little gods always end up tyrants, because deep down the proud heart is an insecure god; it knows it's broken. The proud fear that once you see their brokenness, you'll reject them and leave. Therefore they steal power from you by undermining your self-esteem and shredding your confidence, as well as isolating you from others. They strive to make you believe that they are the only ones who would want you around, and that you are incapable of thinking for yourself or knowing what's true, right, or good apart from them. Psychologists and counselors have often described this kind of person as having a narcissistic personality. Solomon Schimmel writes,

> Like Narcissus, who fell in love with his reflection in a spring and eventually died of frustration because his self-love could never be consummated, the narcissist is totally enamored of himself to the exclusion of interest in the welfare of others. According to Karen Horney, he has an unrealistically idealized self-image which temporarily enhances his self-esteem but which ultimately leads to dissatisfaction when he fails to live up to his glorified vision of himself. The narcissist behaves in ways harmful to both self and society. Many of his features, such as exploitativeness, self-absorption, and dominance, are similar to those of the proud sinner described by the moralists.[3]

Those with proud hearts are always controlling because of their belief that they're always right. Recently, while I was speaking at a women's retreat, a lady in the audience felt compelled to publicly correct a minor misstatement someone made during introductions. Throughout the weekend she was vocally opinionated and seemed oblivious when the other women started to avoid her. Later, she approached me to ask my advice about a problem she was having with her adult daughter—who, in this mother's opinion, was clearly in the wrong. She appeared to want my point of view yet didn't really listen to it, because she merely wanted me to agree with her. She already knew best.

Proud people have many opportunities to see things differently, but seizing these moments requires a degree of humility and the possibility that they are wrong. If you are proud, you may suffer humiliation at times, but an inner posture of humility comes only when you humble *yourself* and realize that you are not God, not always right, not entitled to be first, and not the center of everyone else's world.

God uses circumstances to humble proud hearts, but often instead of acknowledging brokenness and being humbled, the proud heart becomes angry. Lundy Bancroft, in his excellent book *Why Does He Do That?* says, "Abusers carry attitudes that produce fury."[4] Many of the attitudes that Bancroft describes are produced by a heart that believes it is entitled to be served. Pride fuels the angry heart to wrath.

The Angry Heart

> An angry person starts fights;
> a hot-tempered person commits all kinds of sin.
> PROVERBS 29:22

As with pride, not all anger is sinful. God created us to experience a full range of emotions, and, like our other emotions, anger in its healthiest form will inform us something's wrong but will not control us or others.

Allowing our anger to become life-dominating says something about what is going on in our hearts. Paul warns us that angry rages are not a part of our new nature (Ephesians 4:22,31). Anger rises up in us when we are not getting what we want in life—when our wills are thwarted. Even babies express anger when they want to be fed and want it *now*. Arching their backs, they howl not simply, "I'm hungry," but, "I'm hungry *now* and I'm angry that you aren't paying attention to *my* needs this moment."

The toddler who doesn't want to go to bed or desires something from the checkout line at the grocery store collapses to the floor and throws a temper tantrum. No one has to teach these children how to get angry; it just happens. As Christian adults, we don't throw fits to get what we want, do we? In fact, tantrums are not beneath us. James diagnoses the problem of an angry heart when he asks,

> What is causing the quarrels and fights among you? Don't they come from the evil desires at war within you? You want what you don't have, so you scheme and kill to get it (James 4:1-2).

Angry hearts believe they are entitled to use anger as a weapon to get what they want, especially if they believe that what they want is a good thing and they're entitled to it. That was the argument John used to justify his long tirades against Debbie and their children. He wanted respect. He wanted her to be more submissive. He wanted her to pay more attention to the validity of what he was saying. John didn't necessarily want sinful things. But his anger, coupled with his pride, blinded him so that he believed he was entitled to use intimidation and threats to get what he wanted; regardless of the pain it caused his family.

The instinctive wants and desires of our fallen, sinful selves will always interfere with our relationships—with God and others. God in his love for us is always seeking to rearrange the desires of our hearts, for he tells us, "Wherever your treasure is, there the desires of your heart will also be" (Matthew 6:21). He wants and deserves first place! Yet we continue to exchange that truth for a lie and prefer our way over God's way.

Where Change Begins

Jesus tells us that real change doesn't start on the outside, but on the inside. If you are ruled by an angry spirit, learning how to manage your angry outbursts is only a small part of the change you need to make. To rid yourself of your anger, you must look into your heart and reevaluate your treasures. What do you want the most in life?

How we act and live stems from our hearts. Becoming like Jesus requires much more than a change of our outward behaviors. God wants to rearrange the desires of our hearts. Paul tells us, "Those who are dominated by the sinful nature think about sinful things, but those who are controlled by the Holy Spirit think about things that please the Spirit" (Romans 8:5). God wants us to want what he wants and to love him more than we love our own way.

We live in an angry world. Road rage, child abuse, domestic violence, murder, and rape are at all-time highs. Our culture nurtures unhealthy pride, sticking up for one's self at the expense of others, and aggressive competitiveness. Anger impairs our reason. We always feel anger is justified, even righteous, when our individual rights, feelings, perceived needs, and wants are denied. Entitlement thinking fuels the angry heart.

> Of the seven deadly sins, anger is the most pervasive, injurious to self and others, and most responsible for unhappiness and psychopathological behavior. It is also inextricably linked to the other cardinal sins, particularly

pride and envy, as well as to hatred, and it is regularly aroused by frustrated greed and lust.[5]

In the same way that humility pierces through the proud heart, kindness and compassion soften the angry heart. When we feel compassion and practice kindness, we are no longer thinking only of ourselves, but we invest ourselves in the expressed desires, feelings, and wants of another. Cultivating these virtues, which are incompatible with explosive anger, enhances our muscle of self-control. And, as we grow in emotional health, we become better equipped to learn how to control our anger and how to constructively express it when necessary. (We will learn more about how to do that in parts 2 and 3.)

The Envious Heart

> Wherever there is jealousy and selfish ambition,
> there you will find disorder and evil of every kind.
> JAMES 3:16

Unlike good pride or healthy anger, envy is always destructive. Envy arises out of a comparison mind-set. When we look to external characteristics such as beauty, wealth, intelligence, success, and popularity as benchmarks for measuring our own selves, we will feel either better or worse than others. We may think, *You have more than I do. You're prettier, thinner, more popular than I am, and that makes me feel badly about myself and angry with you.* Mark Rutland writes in *Behind the Glittering Mask,*

> Envy is not, as many believe, the simple desire to have what another has. It is the hatred of what another has, or of what another is. Envy is not a longing for more than I have. That is a sin to be sure, but it is not Envy. Envy is the longing for another not to have. Envy is more about depriving than gaining.[6]

Seven Deadly Sins

Envy is related to our pride. It's not so much that we wish we had something, but that we feel angry and inferior because we do not have it, and so we wish to deprive the other person from having it. In the Bible, Cain felt envious that Abel's sacrifice was more acceptable to God. Instead of changing his own sacrifice to be more pleasing to God, Cain murdered his brother (Genesis 4).

King Saul felt jealous when David received more praise and admiration from the people than he did (1 Samuel 18). Initially David and King Saul had a good relationship, but Saul's ego became wounded, and his envy of David grew. King Saul's envy didn't motivate him to do more to enhance his own image with the people; instead, he tried to destroy David.

For the same reasons, the Pharisees wanted Jesus dead. He was impinging on their turf and challenged their authority and influence. Envy breeds contempt, criticism, and hatred of the good in the other person. It tries to reduce or oppose what it cannot attain. In one instance, after Jesus healed someone on the Sabbath, the Pharisees "were wild with rage and began to discuss what to do with him" (Luke 6:11).

How Envy Brings Destruction

Let's look at how envy works in a person's heart, creating turmoil and destruction. Jane was the head of her women's ministry at her church for over 15 years. Jennifer, a newcomer, was eager to get involved in the ministry, and many of the women seemed to respond to her wisdom and insights during their weekly Bible study. Jane found herself feeling jealous of Jenny's easy rapport with the other women and their obvious warmth toward her. Jane had worked long and hard to establish good relationships with her women. How dare a newcomer upstage her ministry! Jane felt consumed with thoughts of Jennifer and grew fearful that the women would soon like Jennifer more than they liked her.

If Jane had been able to recognize and face her threatened pride and her fear of losing the women's admiration, she could have handled her feelings of insecurity much differently. Instead, she was blind to her envy and began to undermine and criticize Jennifer. She would pull Jennifer aside after Bible study and tell her she was being too talkative and that she was offending some of the women with what she said. Jennifer felt shocked by Jane's feedback and began to feel self-conscious in the Bible study. Jane also spoke privately to one of the women in the group known to have trouble keeping her mouth shut. Jane said that she didn't think Jennifer was biblically sound and that they should not be so easily taken in by her charm. It wasn't long before Jennifer began to sense she wasn't welcome. Hurt and sad, she eventually left the church. Jane was unable to affirm Jennifer's gifts because they lessened her. Instead of encouraging Jennifer, she tried to destroy her.

Fairy tales tell stories of envy. The wicked queen envied Snow White's beauty and tried to destroy her. Cinderella's stepsisters and stepmother envied her goodness and sweet spirit and continually mocked and abused her. In tragic real-life instances, I've worked with men and women whose parents so envied their child's gift of beauty, intellect, athleticism, or personality that they could not encourage or praise the child at all. Instead, they continually criticized or demeaned their son or daughter until the child buried that gift entirely.

Envy may destroy another person; unchecked, envy will always destroy you. It is a poison that courses through your veins and will transform you into a resentful, bitter, hateful person. Your mission in life will be to tear others down. We sometimes chuckle and say tongue-in-cheek that so-and-so has the gift of criticism. But one who is chronically critical is a person ruled by envy as well as pride.

Biblical love is the antidote to envy's poison. Paul tells us in 1 Corinthians 13 that love does not envy. In Romans 13, he tells us that love does no harm (verse 10). Love always seeks the other person's good. A wonderful example of someone who loved well, even when he had every human reason to be envious, was Jonathan, King Saul's son. Jonathan was heir to the throne. He saw David's popularity and knew that the prophet Samuel anointed David, not him, to be the next king. However, in spite of his father's envy, Jonathan loved David as much as he loved himself. Jonathan did all he could to protect and bless David (1 Samuel 18:1).

Pride, anger, and envy destroy people and relationships. In the next chapter we will expand our understanding of what makes the heart destructive by looking at the selfish heart, the lazy heart, the evil heart, and the fearful heart.

Destructive Themes of the Heart:
Selfishness, Laziness, Evil, and Fear

*If you want to know what a person really believes,
don't listen to what he says, watch what he does.*

JAMES P. MACKEY

*People will be lovers of themselves, lovers of money,
boastful, proud, abusive, disobedient to their parents,
ungrateful, unholy, without love, unforgiving, slanderous,
without self-control, brutal, not lovers of the good, treacherous,
rash, conceited, lovers of pleasure rather than lovers of God.*

2 TIMOTHY 3:2-4 NIV

The Selfish Heart

They are headed for destruction.
Their god is their appetite, they brag about shameful
things, and they think only about this life here on earth.
PHILIPPIANS 3:19

Each of us struggles with selfish behavior from time to time.
However, a person with a selfish heart is completely captivated by
the triune gods of *me, mine,* and *more.* His lusts, desires, and cravings rule him. *Her* needs, *her* wants, and *her* rights take priority

over anyone else's. A selfish person thinks *I deserve it* and believes the lie *It's all about me.* A person whose heart is self-oriented cannot love well. He is a taker, not a giver. When or if she gives, she is always looking for something in return.

Selfish people want to indulge or consume with little or no thought for the feelings or needs of others who will be affected. (See sidebar for an example from the Bible.) Deception is usually part of the pattern, because selfish people want to avoid the negative consequences of their actions. Other people function as useable objects to meet the desires of the selfish heart. There is no mutual give-and-take in relationships involving a selfish person. When the selfish give, they do so in order to get something or to look good, not because they care about another person's well-being. When that person's needs or desires conflict with theirs, the selfish always come first, and they may become furious if their needs are denied. In his book *The Seven Deadly Sins Today*, Henry Fairlie writes,

> The steps from a reasonable self-concern to an utter selfishness are short and swift. Most of the prescriptions for "self-actualization" today are rationalizations for an aggressive self-centeredness and, in some of their forms, for violent aggression by one's self against other selves that get in the way. If it's not aggression, then it is manipulation, and the end is always the same: striking or maneuvering to take first place.[1]

A TAKER, NOT A GIVER

Amnon, King David's oldest son, exemplifies a person controlled by a selfish heart. Consumed with lust toward his half sister Tamar, Amnon and his friend hatched a plan to fulfill his desire for her. Pretending to be ill, Amnon persuaded his father to ask Tamar to make her special bread for him. Amnon lured Tamar into his bedroom to give him his bread, ordering everyone else to leave. Once alone, Amnon showed his selfish heart by raping Tamar, and when he finished, discarding her like a used tissue (2 Samuel 13).

A selfish person will often call others selfish, because selfish hearts believe that life *is* all about them. One must not require anything of a selfish person, but a selfish person can be very demanding toward others. When Karen told her husband about her dream to return to college after years of being a stay-at-home mother, he replied, "I don't think that's fair. I'm stuck working all day to put you through school? What about me? Who will be here to take care of my needs?"

From Taker to Giver

When the apostle Paul speaks to thieves about their behavior, he does not merely tell them to stop stealing (Ephesians 4:28). Genuine change goes deeper than just stopping destructive behavior, replacing it with loving behavior. A thief has a selfish heart. Stealing is an outward manifestation of his internal greed and selfishness. Paul instructs him to work so that he can share his resources with others who have needs. Paul is talking about the kind of heart change in which a person who used to be a taker now wants to be a giver.

Sally and Rick were working hard to heal from the devastation of Rick's selfishness and deceit. For years, Rick led a double life. He said he loved God. He attended church, served as a deacon, and went on various missions trips. Unknown to Sally, Rick also frequented strip bars, watched pornography, and indulged in one-night stands. When the awful truth finally tumbled out, Rick repented. He desired to change and not only worked diligently on his problem with lust and lack of intimacy, but also began to recognize and repent of his selfish heart.

Recently, he and Sally were on a short vacation. Things had been going well in their relationship, and Rick was hopeful that Sally had put the past behind her. But one day during the trip, she became negative and despondent and Rick blew up. He screamed, "What's wrong with you now? Why do you have to ruin my vacation?" His angry outburst only made matters worse. Later, as we talked about what happened, Rick recognized that his selfish heart, which used to sneak off and indulge in sexual pleasure without consequence, was the same selfish heart that blew up at Sally for "ruining his vacation." Sally and I were encouraged when Rick recognized not only the inappropriateness of his angry outburst, but also the selfishness that fueled it. (A person whose primary orientation is self becomes angry when he doesn't get what he wants—see James 4:1.) Rick still battled selfishness, as we all do, but his blindness to it was gone, and that brought hope to Sally that he was genuinely changing.

The Lazy Heart

> A lazy person is as bad as someone who destroys things.
> PROVERBS 18:9

Biblically, laziness doesn't simply refer to a person who is unwilling to work hard, but to someone who has no meaningful life. The lazy, slothful heart neglects its purpose and worships ease. When we are ruled by laziness, we experience apathy toward life, toward people, and toward God. Fairlie quotes Dorothy Sayers as saying, "It's the sin that believes in nothing, cares for nothing, enjoys nothing, hates nothing, finds purpose in nothing, lives for nothing and remains alive because there is nothing for which it will die."[2]

It is impossible to have a healthy relationship with lazy people. They live for the moment and whatever meaningless pleasure they can snatch from it with as little effort as possible. What attracts a lazy person is what's easiest. Never mind what is best or good or right, those values are unimportant to a lazy heart. Lazy people live their lives as spectators rather than participants. They can spend hours content to watch the real or made-up lives of other people while lounging in an easy chair.

Lazy hearts remain uninterested, uninvolved, and unengaged with others. Lazy hearts disdain the thought that they should care about another person's hurts, burdens, blessings, dreams, and needs, or have to pitch in to help. They want the rewards of life without putting in the hard work to earn them. Cain envied and murdered his brother Abel. Later when God asked Cain where his brother was, he simply shrugged and answered, "I don't know...Am I my brother's guardian?" (Genesis 4:9).

If challenged, lazy people may say they want a good relationship, but they don't want to have to do the work of learning to communicate or give of themselves. They don't want to grow or change. When counseling couples I sometimes hear, "You'll just have to accept me the way I am." What slothful people don't understand, however, is that much of the way they are is extremely unattractive and undesirable. Change would be good not only for the relationship, but also for them. Mark Rutland comments,

> The slothful live and die as spiritual and emotional midgets. They never grow in grace for they cannot endure growth. Growth involves everything that is hateful to the slothful. Pain, patience, diligence, obedience, and discipline are the keys to growth. Yet, for the slothful these are the enemy. They are to be feared, hated and abhorred.[3]

The Results of Sloth

It is amazing to me to observe how surprised people are when they actually reap what they sow (Galatians 6:7-10). Carl and Diane's marriage was over. Diane said she could not continue any longer; their union was dead and she felt devalued by Carl. Carl seemed shocked. He did not want their marriage to be over. He kept reminding Diane that God hates divorce, yet his track record over their 20-year marriage showed no investment of his time or energy in nurturing his wife or their relationship.

Carl had not changed since he and Diane dated in high school. He did not like to talk with her, he did not want to get involved in anything with her, and short of going to occasional sporting events together, he did not want to go anywhere with her. He enjoyed television, sports, beer, and his friends, in that order. He could not understand why Diane couldn't just appreciate that he brought home his paycheck and wasn't mean to her. Although Carl gave lip service to wanting a better marriage, in reality, he expected a loving wife and good marriage with no personal investment on his part. His actions clearly demonstrated that he didn't want to expend any energy improving himself or their relationship.

Any good relationship takes work. It costs to care. In the natural world, what we don't regularly maintain soon deteriorates. If we neglect to water our plants, they die. If we neglect our nails, they get ragged. When we neglect our hygiene, we stink. Why would we expect our relationships to be any different? How can they sustain themselves if we do not nurture them? What makes us think we can neglect the most important thing God calls us to do with our lives (love him and love others), yet reap the benefits of relationship and community? Psychiatrist Scott Peck observes that the main impediment to people's growth is laziness. If we conquer that, he says, all other hurdles can be overcome.[4]

Paul advises us to disassociate from those who are idle. We are not to compensate for those who refuse to carry their load of responsibility, whether financially or relationally. Only when lazy hearts experience the painful consequences of their own sloth will they be enticed to change (2 Thessalonians 3:6).

The Evil Heart

The wicked man craves evil;
his neighbor gets no mercy from him.
PROVERBS 21:10 NIV

Every human heart is inclined toward sin (Romans 3:23), and that includes evil (Genesis 8:21; James 1:14). Even though all of us sin—that is, miss God's mark of moral perfection—most of us do not happily indulge our evil urges, nor do we feel good about having them. We feel ashamed and guilty, and rightly so (Romans 7:19-21). Yet there are those who do not struggle against evil; they delight in it (Proverbs 2:14-15; 10:23). Those who have given themselves over to evil do not experience remorse when they do wicked things, nor do they regret the pain that they inflict. Quite the contrary: it often gives them pleasure to see someone suffer, even if they are quite skillful at hiding their delight.

It is worth noting the difference between foolishness and evil. Foolishness may result in evil and wicked actions, because fools don't think about the consequences of their actions, nor do they anticipate the effects of their behavior on others. They are reckless rather than malicious. The resulting destruction may be similar, but the heart motives are different. Like fools, evil people embrace all types of sins, including those we've covered in these two chapters, yet there is something deeper and more sinister at work in their behaviors as well. The evil heart can be subtly destructive, often disguising itself as good. The foolish heart is usually not that clever.

Choosing and Spreading Ruin

Ken and Mary were separated, yet living in the same house. Everyone who knew them thought Ken was a wonderful father. He seemed to enjoy his children and often took them to special places.

Several months ago, Ken waged war on Mary using the children as his weapons, although no one but Mary witnessed it. Mary had taken her children to church and Sunday school for years, but one Sunday as Mary was getting the kids ready for church, Ken asked, "Hey kids, you want to go to the zoo this morning?" Kids being kids, they chose the zoo.

Ken continued to put their children in the middle by regularly asking them to choose between what their mother told them to do and some appealing place he wanted to take them to. In the evenings, he would interrupt their homework sessions, offering to take them out for ice cream, or he would bring home a video to watch together. When Mary protested, Ken would act as if she was trying to keep him from his children.

"Please, Ken, the kids need to get their homework done," she would say. Or, "Ken, the children need to go to sleep or they won't be rested for school tomorrow." But Ken and the children thought she was being unfair and mean. Kids would always rather play and eat ice cream than go to bed or do homework. That's why God gives them parents. When one of the children did choose to listen to Mary, Ken ignored that child for the rest of the day. If any of the kids showed more loyalty toward their mother than to him, they got the same cold treatment.

Mary could see what was happening. Her children were torn. They obviously enjoyed spending time with their father, but they also were becoming more and more disrespectful toward her. When she tried talking with Ken about how she felt, he told her she was ridiculous. He said, "You're just jealous because I'm a better father than you are a mother, and the kids know it. I love my children and I want to spend as much time as I can with them. What's wrong with that?" Mary felt speechless. How could she argue?

The Greek words for *evil* denote both heart intent and outward behaviors. However, one word, *kakós,* indicates one who "may be content to perish in his own corruption," while the other word, *ponērós* (a name also attributed to Satan in Matthew 6:13 and Ephesians 6:16), describes a person who "is not content unless he is corrupting others as well and drawing them into the same destruction with himself."[5]

Psychologist Dan Allender observes,

> One awful, abusive event does not make a person evil, but when it represents a repetitive pattern of excessive disregard for others (mockery) and a wanton, vicious refusal to look at the damage done (arrogance), then one can ascertain a significant inclination to evil.[6]

Evil is cunning and deceptive, because evil originates with the

Evil One. It can be extremely difficult to discern evil hearts, because their intention is to look good, not be good. The serpent appeared beautiful; he seemed genuinely interested in Eve's welfare. Had he shown his true colors, she would have felt afraid and never had a conversation with him. Evil people want to look good to others; they also want to appear good in their own eyes so that the pangs of healthy shame and self-reproach do not penetrate their hearts.

Paul instructs us not to be passive toward an evil person. He says we are to overcome evil with good (Romans 12:21). What that looks like and how to do it will be covered in parts 2 and 3.

The Fearful Heart

> Fear of man will prove to be a snare,
> but whoever trusts in the LORD is kept safe.
> PROVERBS 29:25 NIV

A look at the destructive aspects of our inner worlds would be incomplete without addressing the heart issue that people struggle with most: All individuals in destructive relationships have fearful hearts. They are afraid of seeing truth, afraid of being hurt, afraid of loss, afraid of being wrong, afraid of rejection, afraid of conflict, afraid of change, afraid of being alone, afraid they might not have what it takes to succeed, afraid to be loved, afraid to give love, afraid they might not be adequate or desirable or loveable.

Because of some or all of these fears, anxious people may pretend, placate, and please, or threaten, manipulate, dominate, and abuse others in the hope that, if they can successfully control others or life, their deepest fears won't come true. Their mission is not usually malicious but self-protective. They cannot love well and are destructive toward both themselves and others.

Being authentic and truthful isn't easy for most people. Our fears of rejection keep us pretending and hiding (especially in the area of our feelings, thoughts, and desires). Instead of having freedom to be and become who God made us to be, we strive to be who we think the other person wants us to be. We want the other person to like us, stay with us. When fearful hearts hide and pretend, however, they forfeit the opportunity for genuine intimacy. They can never feel deeply loved, because deep down they know that the person other people love is not the person they truly are.

Relationally fearful people don't want to be gods, like the proud person does, but they allow their lives to be ruled by others instead of God. They give the god substitutes power, power to define them and their worth. They bow to the people gods in order to keep what they fear losing.

When you place your entire worth and well-being into the hands of a person instead of God, you give that person the power to destroy you.

Snared by Fear

Fran called me in tears. Her husband just announced he was leaving her for a woman he'd met on the Internet. This wasn't the first time he'd had an affair. Fran wasn't sure she could go through this again. His behavior was killing her. Yet, over the years, despite being counseled to stand firm and set boundaries that would encourage her husband to realize his own brokenness, Fran kept allowing Jack to move back home when his other relationships failed, because she was afraid to be without him.

Jack was self-centered and bowed to the idol of pleasure and lust. Fran centered herself on her husband. He became her god, and she bowed to whatever he wanted in order to not lose him. Functionally, he was her life, and she couldn't bear the thought of being alone. Yet in her insecurity and fear, she also attempted to control Jack. She would obsessively check his computer, his cell phone, and car for signs that he was being unfaithful. When she found evidence of his relationships with other women, she would unleash her anger and pain by threatening to hurt herself, hoping Jack would feel guilty enough to stay with her.

Unless Fran dethrones her husband as the god of her life and stops giving him the power of life and death over her emotions, she will never gain the strength or courage to break the destructive cycle in her marriage. The psychological term is <u>codependent</u> and the lie is, *I NEED you to love me* or *I NEED you to need me in order to make me feel alive and worthy.* People who believe this lie are caught in emotionally destructive relationships because their first love is a sinful mortal and not the true God.

When we live to protect ourselves from relational pain, we cannot live freely or authentically. Instead of surrendering to God, people governed by fear surrender to their emotions, surrender to people, and surrender to lies, forcing themselves to live according to their false selves. Christian psychologist David Benner says, "The core of the false self is the belief that my value depends on what I have, what I can do and what others think of me."[7] When we bow to these false gods and believe lies, we cannot become what God intended. We only grow into our true selves as we surrender to the reality of God's unfailing love for us and his purposes for our life. To do that, we have to let go of our small lives governed by false gods (Matthew 10:38-39; 16:24-25). How to do this will be explained more fully in part 3.

> ## SAFETY IN TRUSTING GOD
>
> God tells us over and over and over again, "Do not be afraid, trust me" (see, for example, Isaiah 41:10-13; 43:1). Jesus says the same thing when he tells us not to let our hearts become troubled or anxious (see Matthew 10:31; Mark 5:36; John 14:27). The Bible tells us that "perfect love expels all fear" (1 John 4:18). It's not our love for God that keeps us from fear, but *his* perfect love for *us*. Believing that God deeply loves us and is for us changes us (Romans 8). Embracing this truth replaces our anxious hearts with peace and trust, because we realize that God is the only one able to love us perfectly. (See Psalm 56:3; Philippians 4:6-8; Colossians 3:15.) Knowing God's love experientially is a process all of us are growing into. Without that anchor, we will be ruled by fear.

The Changed Heart

If you've read chapters 4 and 5 and don't recognize yourself battling any of these heart sins, but you know you have littered your past with a trail of broken relationships or people, stop right now and ask God to search your heart and show you what's wrong (Psalm 139:23-24). Remember, your unwillingness to see truth about yourself has been your biggest obstacle to having healthy, loving relationships. You may want to ask those closest to you to be honest with you and tell you what they see going on in your heart. Though you may be surprised and feel hurt by what they share, don't shrink back from the truth. It is essential for your well-being that you face your own blindness and lies so that you can move toward greater emotional, spiritual, and relational wholeness.

Our destructive relational partners aren't the only guilty parties. When we're honest with ourselves, we readily recognize some of these attitudes within *our* hearts. Don't despair. We all struggle with idolatry, lies, and sin. Recognizing what controls our hearts and naming it biblically is a good first step. Change can only happen when we stop being blind to what's going on in our own hearts. Whenever we are controlled by *I want, I need, I think, I feel, I deserve, I'm afraid,* or *I'm entitled to,* we're prone to sin. I'm not saying that being aware of the things we want, need, think, or feel is wrong or selfish. Quite the contrary: Awareness is an essential element of good mental and spiritual health. However, when what we want, feel, think, or need takes first place and rules our hearts, we're prone to deception, as we will be whenever we put anything ahead of God and his truth.

Why so much emphasis on our hearts? Because God says our hearts affect everything else we do:

> *My child, pay attention to what I say.*
> *Listen carefully to my words.*
> *Don't lose sight of them.*
> *Let them penetrate deep into your heart,*

> *for they bring life to those who find them,*
> *and healing to their whole body.*
> *Guard your heart above all else,*
> for it determines the course of your life.
>
> —PROVERBS 4:20-24

Genuine change requires a transformed heart. That's why it's so important to expect repentance to involve more than a change in outward behaviors. Someone can act nice but still be motivated by a selfish or fearful heart. Destructive behavior is merely the outward fruit of a deeper root that must be identified and uprooted.

Please note that genuine repentance doesn't mean that we never do destructive or sinful things anymore. What it does mean is that when our hearts change, we no longer *want* to do those things, nor are we blind to them. We see them as evil, hurtful, sinful, and destructive, and want to be free from them. We no longer justify them, excuse them, indulge them, or pamper them. Now we slay them.

I'm often asked if it is hard to change these patterns. I won't lie to you. It takes work. It's painful to give up old ways of thinking, feeling, and relating. However, I try to impart to my clients this important lesson: If we don't choose the pain of hard work and discipline required to change, we will later face the pain of regret for not changing. The choice is ours to make. My prayer is that you (and your partner) courageously choose the path of change.

Part Two

Stopping It

6

The Truth About Change: You Can Stop Living This Way

It may be hard for an egg to turn into a bird;
it would be a jolly sight harder for it to learn to fly
while remaining an egg. We are like eggs at present.
And you cannot go on indefinitely being just an ordinary,
decent egg. We must be hatched or go bad.

C.S. Lewis

Wisdom will save you from evil people,
from those whose words are twisted.

Proverbs 2:12

C ynthia called me, frantic. "I can't take it anymore," she said. Her husband had closed their mutual checking account and put everything into his name. She was required to submit to him an itemized list for everything she purchased, with all the receipts. When she asked him why he would do this to her, he told her it was his money and he could do what he wanted. She should just "shut up" and "get off his back." Cynthia's husband disrespected her and refused to treat her as an equal partner. He sabotaged her relationship with her children by undermining her authority, contradicting her discipline of them, and speaking disrespectfully about her to them. By the time she finally came for counseling, she was a mess.

"I don't know what to do, Leslie," she cried. "How do I learn to live like this? I'm trying to obey God and be a good wife and mother, but I can't take it. I'm afraid I'm going to have a nervous breakdown."

After listening to Cynthia describe her life over the past few years, I gently suggested to her that perhaps God didn't want her to learn to live like this at all. Perhaps God wanted to give her the strength to look at her situation differently so she might gain the wisdom and courage to confront her husband's controlling behaviors and disrespectful attitudes toward her.

Cynthia hesitated. She wasn't sure she could do that. I knew what was coming next. She let out a deep sigh and said, "I guess, then, there's nothing I can do. I'll just have to figure out how to accept my miserable life."

Cynthia's response to my suggestions didn't surprise me. Even if she knew what to do, at the time she was too afraid to do it. Sometimes, however dysfunctional, sinful, or unhappy a relationship is, maintaining the status quo often seems preferable to rocking the boat and risking having your world turned upside down.

⟶

Throughout parts 2 and 3, I will extensively cover how to gain greater emotional and spiritual health for yourself and your relationships. First, though, let me introduce a few basic guidelines for taking the first steps needed to stop the destructiveness.

Facing Reality

Before Cynthia was ready to tackle a discussion with her husband, she needed a better understanding of what God says about relationships and of what she is and is not responsible for in her marriage. In the past, Cynthia had read good books about destructive and abusive relationships, but she felt too afraid and too guilty to take any action, because she believed that God wanted her to stay with her husband no matter what. What was she to do? What choices did she have?

I hope you see by now how lying to yourself is so detrimental to your well-being. When we habitually deceive ourselves we cannot grow or mature in a godly way. (Please review the discussion of this in chapter 3 if you need to.) As painful as truth can be, we must face it if we want to become healthy, no matter how much we don't like what it tells us.

Recently a woman e-mailed me about her experience:

> I believe that getting out of a destructive situation has nothing to do with recognizing that the other person is abusive or that we are not safe, or in getting the other person to change. I believe that I began to change when I realized that my life was spiraling downward and I felt hopeless. I realized that the choices I'd made over and over again were not getting me closer to joy but were taking me further and further down a destructive road. Recovery came for me when *I decided that I needed to change,* and that I was the only person I could affect or change, and that I couldn't do this alone. I needed God.[1]

Like Cynthia and this woman, as well as all the other men and women I've described thus far, the most painful step in any healing process is often the first one. You must face the ugly truth that you're in a destructive relationship and that you are the one who has allowed it to continue. Just like a person wouldn't begin chemotherapy unless she first accepted that she has cancer, you will not take the steps necessary to grow, heal, or change if you are still in denial. As long as you minimize the truth about your problem, you cannot become strong enough to challenge or change anything.

You might be further along in your journey than Cynthia was and may have already taken this first step. Others, like Cynthia, are just waking up to the awful reality of how destructive their relationships truly are. Wherever you are, it is important you realize that stopping the destructive dance starts with you. Here are some things that you can do right now to begin the process of facing reality.

You Can Pray

Talking with God about what's happening both in your own heart as well as in your circumstances is important for many reasons, not the least of which is that you are about to battle an enemy much larger and vastly more powerful than your partner. Jesus called Satan a destroyer and the Father of Lies (John 8:44; 10:10). His aim is to shatter your spirit, demolish your soul, and wreck everything good in your life.

You must become aware of his tactics, because words are his primary weapon. He hurls accusations, slander, lies, half truths, and even phrases or passages from the Bible (taken out of context) to confuse, manipulate, distract, and devastate you. Satan uses people to accomplish his purposes, just like he used Judas to betray Jesus and tried to use Peter to distract Christ from his mission (Matthew 16:22-23). Satan may be influencing your partner or even using your partner to destroy you, but don't let him! Prayer protects us, and prayer changes us. It also helps us guard our hearts against our own lies, excuses, rationalizations, and fears.

God gives us our own arsenal of weapons with which to fight our enemies, but God's weapons are not the same kind that the world uses. The apostle Paul said that prayer unleashes divine power to take down strongholds and demolish false arguments (2 Corinthians 10:4). Paul also instructs us to put on our spiritual armor daily, and to learn how to wield the sword of truth to fight evil. (See Ephesians 6:10-18, as well as Matthew 4 and Luke 4, which show how Jesus used God's Word to counter Satan's attacks.) Prayer provides a shield of protection so that neither Satan nor people can destroy your spirit, even if they are successful at injuring you (Matthew 10:28).

Prayer sometimes changes us more than it changes our situations:

- It teaches us to look at our circumstances from a much larger vantage point than what is dictated by our immediate needs or anxieties.

- It reminds us that God is in control, even when we feel like evil is winning (Psalm 118:5-6).

- It teaches us to reflect upon our lives as well as our dilemmas from God's perspective, so that we are better equipped to best address the destructive person, recognize our own complicity, and handle the situation we're in without sinning or becoming more destructive ourselves.

Ask God to rescue you from wicked and evil people. (Read David's prayer in Psalm 140 and the apostle Paul's instruction in 2 Thessalonians 3:2.) God deeply cares for those who feel impotent against powerful people and those who have been mistreated or oppressed. Jesus knows how you feel. He too was mocked, humiliated, taunted, rejected, lied about, and beaten. He wept over the indifference of the Jews and the blindness of the Pharisees because he longed to have a different kind of relationship with them.

Learn to run quickly to him when you're hurting, confused, angry, or tempted. He is faithful to help us (Hebrews 4:15-16).

You Can Disclose What's Happening

When you're in a destructive relationship, especially if it's your marriage, you may feel ashamed and may isolate yourself from sources of support because you don't want anyone to know how bad your situation really is. You may also want to protect your spouse from having others think negatively about him or her. Even though Cynthia wasn't ready to make any changes, she took a first step toward ending the destructive cycle when she admitted to me out loud the way her husband treated her. Putting your experiences and feelings into words helps you *see* more clearly what's really going on.

Appropriate disclosure isn't an opportunity to bad-mouth another person or to gossip, but to avoid the harm that always comes to people who hold destructive secrets. The apostle Paul encourages us not to participate in the unfruitful deeds of darkness, but rather to expose them (Ephesians 5:11). If you are being emotionally abused or physically or sexually mistreated, it is good to tell someone. In his book *Healing of Memories,* Christian counselor David Seamands reminds us that once you say something out loud in front of another person, it's much harder to continue to deny it to yourself.[2]

Sharing your situation with someone is a big step. If nothing else, a confidant can pray with you for wisdom and courage to make the changes you need to make. If you've tried telling someone and were not heard, believed, or were told that the situation is your fault, don't give up. Find someone else. Not everyone is knowledgeable or equipped to wisely and compassionately handle these kinds of disclosures.

You Can Ask for Support

Jesus tells us in Matthew 18:15-17 that when someone hurts us, we should first talk privately with that person about what he or she has done. (How to do this will be covered in chapter 8.) But when our efforts fall on deaf ears, Jesus encourages us to enlist the help of one or two others as advocates and witnesses. God knows that some things are too difficult and dangerous to do alone.

Facing conflict or having to make changes is not easy for anyone. God never asks us to live without support and help from others. Through dialogue with trusted and wise people, we often learn how to label our problems correctly and work toward solutions that are consistent with biblical principles.

Much of the New Testament instructs us on how to encourage, love, and care for other people, especially those in need or facing difficult situations. Don't shy away from asking for someone to help bear your burdens even though it's difficult to ask (Galatians 6:2). Getting support is one of the best steps you can make to regain some personal control over your life.

We all need support, accountability, and a specific plan when we're trying to make changes. When we know that we're heard, believed, affirmed, and cared about, we gain confidence and grow more quickly than when we attempt it all alone. A Jewish proverb wisely states, "Sticks in a bundle are not easily broken; sticks alone can be broken by a child." Part of your change and growth will involve finding and making new friends and building healthier relationships.

"I had so much fun this weekend," Emily told me during our session after she attended a women's retreat at her church. "The ladies actually liked me and told me I was fun to be around."

At the retreat, Emily experienced people who described her differently than her husband did. As Emily gets to know this new group of women better, hopefully she will find one or two whom she can ask to pray for and encourage her as she gathers up the courage to have a difficult discussion with her husband.

If you're involved in a home group, Bible study, or Sunday school class, you might know specific individuals or couples whom you can ask to pray for you, encourage you, and hold you accountable for making the changes you desire to make. You don't always have to disclose all the details of your situation to ask for prayer or specific help. If you're not involved in a church, ask a friend, sibling, grandparent, neighbor, or other wise and godly person to support you right now. You can do this even if you aren't sure how to best approach your destructive relationship just yet. Often we can more easily identify the lies that we've believed and gain the strength to break free from them *after* we are well connected to other people.

Right now, stop reading and think of three people whom you

**IF YOU'RE
HELPING SOMEONE**

If you are a person someone has con-
fided in, asking for support and help,
please be careful. People in destructive
relationships are wounded and broken
people (as we all are, but their wounds
are usually more visible). But if you are
not familiar with the dynamics of these
kinds of relationship patterns, you
might unintentionally give bad advice
or hurt the person more. Please read
"A Special Word to People Helpers"
at the back of this book to learn some
specific ways you can listen well and
be of help.

could ask to pray for you and encourage you as you grow through this process. If you can't think of anyone, don't despair. A recent study indicated that the average American has only two close confidants, and one in four has no close friends at all.[3] If that is the case for you, you are lacking an ingredient necessary for good emotional and spiritual health and can begin to change this immediately. How? Get involved somewhere. Join a group, participate in a church or ministry, volunteer, go to lunch with your co-workers.

Take the time to reread the characteristics of a healthy relationship in chapter 1 and promise yourself that you will learn how to recognize healthy, mature individuals. As you see these traits in others, invite them to be a part of your life.

You Can Name and Face Your Fears

You probably already felt afraid when I advised you to ask someone to help support you. You might be thinking, *What if they say no? Then what will I do? I'll feel like a jerk. No one wants to help me. I'm not worth it. I don't deserve it. No one even likes me.*

If you felt this way, fear is a large part of your life. I know that, because if you weren't so afraid you would have already taken steps to break the destructive cycle of your relationship. Perhaps you're afraid of conflict or rejection. Maybe it's your fear of failure, fear of being alone, fear of hurting someone's feelings, or fear of getting hurt that stops you cold. These are just a few of the many fears that I, as well as the people I've counseled, have felt in similar situations.

In order to become healthier, however, we must begin to face what we are most afraid of and walk through it instead of allowing it to control us. When fear grabs hold of us, we shrink back and become smaller. We're afraid to make a mistake, so we won't push ourselves in difficult areas. We don't want to look stupid, so we don't try things that we might actually enjoy, like teaching a class, dancing, or singing in the choir. We're afraid we'll make people upset, so we don't speak our true feelings; instead we stuff them. We're afraid of being wrong, so we don't offer up our ideas or opinions—then we never get to see if our ideas are helpful or interesting to another person, and soon we don't even remember what they were.

Before moving on, take a minute right now to write down what you think your biggest fears are. Why haven't you taken some action about this destructive relationship you're stuck in? What are you afraid of?

When I asked Joyce this question about her relationship with her older sister, she said, "If I tell her how hurt I feel when she talks to me that way, I'm afraid that she won't care. I'm afraid that I won't matter. I'm afraid that she would sooner walk away from our relationship than change. I don't want to lose her. She's my only sister."

Our fears aren't always imaginary. Joyce's sister might not care. She might walk away rather than listen to Joyce's feelings. However, what's the alternative? Joyce isn't happy that her big sister uses her when she needs something but otherwise is aloof and bitingly sarcastic. Change *does* involve risk, and that is scary for most of us. But living without risk does not mean we'll be free of pain, nor does living without fear mean we have to become reckless and calloused. If Joyce wants to stop her painful encounters with her sister, she will need to face her fears before she will be strong enough to initiate healthy change.

If the prospect of an honest conversation with someone who hurts you is too scary right now, start facing your fears by taking smaller risks. Look over your list of the kinds of things you're afraid of and pick one or two to work on. For example, if you're afraid you might disappoint someone, return an item you received as a gift without making a big deal out of it. If you're afraid to ask someone for what you want or tell someone what you don't like, try implementing some small-scale ventures. For example, when dining out, ask to have your entrée prepared without fats or oils if you'd like it that way, or send it back if it's not prepared the way you asked. Call up a friend and ask him out for lunch, or be bold and tell a telemarketer that you do not want to listen to his sales pitch.

If you're afraid you will feel stupid and so hold yourself back, do something silly or foolish like deliberately singing out loud in a crowded elevator. What happened? Nothing! You lived through it. So you felt stupid; you also felt freer somehow.

We learn to live differently by living differently, not by thinking about living differently. We must take action against our fears. In our brokenness, fear will never completely leave us, but we can stop fear from controlling us.

You Can Replace Lies with God's Truth

When we are caught up in destructive relationship patterns, it's often hard to sort out what is destructive, what is normal, what is justified, what is sin, or what is unhealthy. Working with individuals caught in the web of destructive relationships, I have seen the power of lies and half truths. They not only wreak havoc over one's emotional life, but they can also decimate one's personhood. That's why it is so vital we all sharpen our ability to discern truth from lies and half truths. What you believe to be true (whether or not it *actually* is true), forms an interpretative lens over what we perceive about ourselves, our lives, God, and what happens to us. Belief defines reality for us.

For example, as we saw in chapter 4, a person with a proud and selfish heart believes that he is entitled to have his needs met first. He believes that he is better than others are. Because of that mind-set, when his wife is busy doing something that she needs to do instead of attending to his needs, he interprets her as being intentionally hurtful or disrespectful. He thinks to himself, *How dare she put me off?* Subsequently, he feels enraged.

In contrast, a person with a humble heart would not feel hurt or interpret his wife's busyness as disrespect. Instead of reacting angrily, he might even offer to help her. He responds differently because he perceives her differently. He does not believe he's more important than she is or that everyone should put his needs first or cater to him.

The apostle Paul says that one of the ways we mature is by renewing our minds with the truth (Romans 12:2). Remember, the Bible teaches us that we naturally lean into lies or half truths because of our own brokenness. Healing starts when we become mindful about what we think, what we are telling ourselves, or what someone else is telling us, then hold it under the light of the truth of God's Word. Then we can see more clearly and compare what we think or believe with what God says is true, good, and right.

Actually doing this is not simple. Lies often *feel* more powerful and true than God's Word does. I remember speaking with a woman who was an intelligent, competent, professional person. Her husband told her that she was stupid. He said this so often she began to believe him and eventually quit her nursing career for a job far beneath her skill level.

When I asked her how he convinced her she was stupid when it was obvious that she wasn't, she replied, "A line from the movie *Pretty Woman* says it best: 'When people put you down enough, you start to believe it. The bad stuff is easier to believe about yourself.'"

Learning to identify lies and embrace the truth is a continual and ongoing process until the day we die. It is best to do this work in community with other believers who seek God's truth, because when we observe that others fall down in the same ways we do, we realize we're not so alone or totally messed up.

UNDERSTANDING BIBLICAL AUTHORITY, HEADSHIP, AND SUBMISSION

As I've worked with Christians in the midst of relationship difficulties, I've identified some specific mistruths and half truths that are sometimes taught as God's truth. Some individuals misuse God's Word and take it out of context to justify or excuse their own sin and brokenness. Some of the teaching that has most powerfully fueled many destructive relationships emerges from the topic of submission to authority, whether it be in a marriage, church, or government.

God's Word gives specific instructions to those in authority on how to handle that responsibility. Throughout the Old Testament, God often rebuked the leaders of Israel for their self-centered, deceitful, and abusive shepherding of God's flock. (See, for example, Deuteronomy 13; Jeremiah 23:1-4; Ezekiel 34:2-4.)

Parents have authority over their children, but, fathers (and mothers by implication) are warned by Paul not to misuse that authority by provoking their children or exasperating them. Paul says the hearts of mistreated children will be tempted with anger, discouragement, and bitterness (Ephesians 6:4; Colossians 3:21). In other words, parents don't have the right to mistreat, demean, or micromanage their children under the guise of biblical discipline.

Biblically, God put husbands as the head over their wives (Ephesians 5:23), but that does not put wives at the feet of their husbands. Women and wives are depicted in the Gospel as equal partners and persons to love, not objects to use or property to own. Biblical headship is modeled by Christ's gentle leadership and loving self-sacrifice. Husbands are cautioned not to be harsh with their wives and not to mistreat them, or their prayers will be hindered (Colossians 3:19; 1 Peter 3:7). No leader is entitled to make selfish demands, order people around, or hurt them when they fail.

Submission is a discipline of the heart for all believers to practice, not just wives or women. All Christians are called to submit to authority (1 Peter 2:13), to one another (Ephesians 5:21), and to God (James 4:7). But don't misunderstand what submission is and what it is not. In the Greek, the word *submission (hupotassō)* describes a voluntary action or attitude. Biblical submission cannot be forced. It is a position we take when we are motivated by our love for Christ and our desire to please and obey him. Although God commands us to submit to him, obey him, and love him, he never forces anyone to comply with his commands. He gives us a free choice, including freedom to choose badly (like Adam and Eve did).

When a husband bullies his wife, his behavior does not describe biblical headship, nor is her forced "submission" characteristic of biblical submission.[4] The correct terms are *coercion, manipulation, intimidation,* or *rape*—and she is the *victim.* Let's make sure we use the right words.

I am amazed by those instances when a man who believes strongly in forcible submission is confronted with his own sin but is unwilling to submit himself to anyone else's authority for help and accountability, including his own pastor. Such a man is not open to correction, challenge, or change because he is always right. He manipulates the Scriptures to serve his purposes.

Jesus cautions those in positions of authority—parents, husbands, pastors, and elders—not to misuse those God-ordained positions for self-centered purposes. These roles are given to us by God to humbly serve the individuals or groups that have been entrusted to our care, not to have our egos stroked or to get our own way (Mark 10:42-45).

Sadly, some husbands have used their God-given position in their homes for selfish purposes, and often other Christians have unwittingly endorsed them. These husbands believe they have license to do or demand anything they want, and that their wives are supposed to comply. This ought not to be.

If you are in a destructive relationship with a person who misuses his or her authority, whether it be your husband, parent, employer, pastor, or government, God gives us specific instructions on how to respond. The following are some things you can do to stop the destruction.

Respect the authority, if not the behavior. When Paul defended himself before the Sanhedrin, Ananias, the high priest, ordered that Paul be slapped across the mouth. Paul reacted to this by calling Ananias a hypocrite and telling him that God would strike him. When Paul was informed that he had insulted the high priest, Paul immediately felt remorse, because he knew God had said, "You must not speak evil of any of your rulers." Paul continued to defend his position before the Sanhedrin, but he presented his point of view with an attitude of respect for Ananias's position (see Acts 23:1-9).

It is tempting to repay insult for insult, evil for evil. God tells us that that is not his way, and this approach will never stop the destruction (Luke 6:27-36; 1 Peter 3:9). Instead we must learn to speak the truth, always in love, without backing down (Ephesians 4:15). Specific examples of how to do this will be given in chapters 8 and 9.

Protect yourself. When David was being mistreated by King Saul, he didn't submit to the mistreatment or wait around for Saul to kill him. He fled. Later, when David had opportunity to ambush and kill King Saul, he refused to, out of respect for Saul's authority and position (1 Samuel 24:6). It is never wrong or against God's will to protect yourself by fleeing from those who misuse their power and authority.

An angel warned Joseph in a dream to take baby Jesus and flee to Nazareth (Matthew 2:19-21). Joseph did not hesitate, nor did he wait for Herod to kill Jesus. Paul was lowered in a basket over a city wall to get away from those who wanted to stone him (Acts

9:23-25). Proverbs tells us, "A prudent man sees danger and takes refuge" (22:3 NIV). If you are in a dangerous situation, get out.

Allow higher authorities to be your advocate. After preaching in Rome, the apostle Paul was mocked and threatened. The Roman commander ordered Paul arrested and beaten. Paul did not submit to this mistreatment. He appealed and questioned whether it was lawful for them to flog a Roman citizen without a proper trial (see Acts 22:22-29).

Whenever people ask me if they should call the police when someone, even a spouse, physically or sexually mistreats them, I say *yes!* It is biblical to rely on the governing authorities God has put in place to protect you against abusive people or those who are misusing their positions of authority or disobeying the law (Romans 13:1-5).

If you are in a situation where you are experiencing sexual harassment or abuse in your workplace, report these practices to someone who has authority over the abusive person. People often act aggressively and abusively toward others primarily because they think they can get away with it. Don't let them. Do not feel guilty about holding someone who is sinning against you accountable to the law. It is not only good for you to do this; it is good for the sinner as well (James 5:19-20).

You can choose to stop living in a destructive cycle. By taking small steps, you can mark the beginning of the end. Is this something you want badly enough to begin? If you decide to allow yourself to be drawn repeatedly into these kinds of destructive relationships, you must ask yourself what part you play in these situations. The point of naming your own complicity is not to make you feel bad, but rather to empower you to stop.

When you face your part and refuse to live as merely a helpless victim, you will find the strength to take back some control over your life. If you continue being passive and blind or refuse to take ownership, you set yourself up to be victimized again and again. Don't do it. You can stop living this way!

7

The Truth About Choices:
They Have Not Been Taken from You

The things that hurt, instruct.

Benjamin Franklin

Do not despise these small beginnings,
for the LORD rejoices to see the work begin.

Zechariah 4:10

~~~

Taking responsibility for yourself is a big step toward good mental, emotional, and spiritual growth. To take responsibility for our own actions does not necessarily mean we take full blame for something, although this is exactly why many of us avoid taking responsibility. We equate it with having to say that the destructive nature of our relationships is entirely our fault.

Perhaps a more helpful way of thinking about responsibility is to call it *ownership*. Cynthia (from the last chapter) hates her miserable life, but she will not *own* it. From her perspective, misery is something that is happening *to* her, and she believes she has no control over it or power to change it. But that is not entirely true. Cynthia has no power to change her husband, nor can she alone make her marriage work, but she *can* exercise her will to make some crucial choices.

For starters, Cynthia could choose to speak up to her husband and tell him that his way of handling their family money is unacceptable to her. She could choose not to engage in a discussion with him unless he is willing to listen to her perspective and feelings. She could go out and get a job to generate her own income. She could decide to live with her husband's control over her and make the best of it, or she could choose to hate it and grow more and more angry and resentful. She could also initiate a temporary separation so that her husband might recognize his abusive behavior and stop. These are a few of the obvious decisions she could make in her particular situation.

What often stops us from taking responsibility or ownership in a situation is that we don't see our choices, or perhaps more truthfully we don't *like* our choices. They feel wrong, unacceptable, or just plain hard. Cynthia didn't want a separation. She didn't know how to speak up. She didn't think it was best to work and leave her children in day care. None of her options look good to her. They look hard, negative, and painful. They seem overwhelming and impossible.

Whenever we face a lack of appealing choices, we feel helpless and may become paralyzed and do nothing. However, when we make no decision, we must own our choice to be passive. I'm not saying that choosing to be passive is a wrong choice—at certain times it might be the best choice—but you must understand that passivity often leads to becoming a repeat victim or a resentful martyr.

Throughout the rest of this chapter, we will look at ways you can own your life so that you can begin to stop the destruction. This process begins when you can accept responsibility for what *you* are doing and who *you* are becoming.

Take Responsibility for Your Choices

As Cynthia must learn for herself, taking responsibility for your life begins when you recognize that you have the power to make choices. If you have been or are in a controlling or abusive relationship, your partner has robbed you of your right to choose from certain options, and indeed you may feel like you have no choices at all. But Viktor Frankl, psychologist and Nazi death-camp survivor, powerfully reminds us in his book *Man's Search for Meaning* that we always have choices, even when they are limited:

> We who lived in concentration camps can remember the men who walked through the huts comforting others, giving away their last piece of bread. They may have been few in number, but they offer sufficient proof that everything can be taken from a man but one thing: the last of the human freedoms—to choose one's attitude in any given set of circumstances, to choose one's own way.[1]

When we surrender *all* of our decision-making power to another, we are either extremely sick or unconscious (physically, mentally, spiritually, or emotionally). Many healthy individuals set up a living will just to ensure that they don't lose their choices regarding their physical care if they should become incapacitated. If you have allowed someone to take your decision-making power from you, you must reclaim it if you want to get healthy. Your will is one of God's gifts to you, and a good relationship with someone is impossible when one of you lacks the power to choose.

Don't Choose to Assume Responsibility for Others

If you are the controlling person in the relationship, your practice of manipulating, threatening, intimidating, harassing, or using guilt to get people to do something they really don't want to do will never secure the love or emotional connection you want from them. These behaviors actually will create more insecurity for you, because the people in relationship with you will stop speaking about their true feelings. They will bury problems that you could have worked through together, problems that will certainly resurface in ways you may not anticipate.

Debra caught her husband using pornography. She also knew he ogled attractive women during church and when they went out together. Any woman in Debra's situation would feel hurt, angry, and insecure. "Aren't I pretty enough?" she cried to Sam. "What's wrong with me that you want to stare at other women?"

Instead of allowing Sam to take responsibility for his problem with sexual lust, Debra took responsibility for him. She told him he was not allowed to use the computer when she was not there and put a password on it to ensure that he could not. Whenever they went out together, she told him to focus his eyes downward so that he wouldn't be tempted to look at a pretty woman and lust after her. Sam was not allowed to watch television without Debra present and holding onto the remote control so that she could change the channel if objectionable content came up. Any of these tactics might be appropriate had Sam chosen them for himself, but Debra's controlling behavior only masked her husband's lust.

What compelled Debra to micromanage her husband's life? Her fears and insecurities for sure. Unless Debra owns those fears as her problem and works on them (rather than on her husband), she won't mature.

Ask Yourself Why

Ask yourself what makes you choose to say yes to people when you want to say no? What are you afraid will happen if you say no? When you're upset, why do you choose to calm down by drinking too much alcohol or overeating instead of asking for help or doing something constructive about your feelings? As painful as the process will feel, it is important at this point to ask yourself why you make the choices you do, even if you're choosing to do nothing. What's the reason you choose to stay in a relationship where you are mistreated, disrespected, or ignored? You might have a good reason or a poor reason. At this juncture, the goal is for you to become aware of those reasons, not to beat yourself up over them.

It is important for you to grasp that every choice we make has consequences, some immediate and others long-term. At times our choices feel right in the moment, but later we reap regret. Debra chose to control Sam's computer time because it made her feel less anxious for the moment, but in the long run she gained no more confidence in Sam's heart. Controlling other people is like putting them in prison. They can't wander away, but you worry what would happen if you unlocked the door.

On the other hand, a decision that looks difficult in the moment might yield the greatest good in the long run. For example, during one of her husband's tirades, Jeri locked herself in the bathroom. He banged down the door, and she chose to call the police. She eventually chose to move out and separate in the hopes that he would see he needed help for his temper. These decisions were the most difficult of her life. Her pastor rebuked her for involving secular authorities, and her church friends rejected her, but Jeri and her children were safe and over the next few months began thriving.

FREE TO CHOOSE

Our tendency to stick with old patterns points back to our brokenness (see chapter 3). Because of the fall, our human nature is prone to believing lies and making ourselves, things, or other people into gods in our life. But there is good news: Jesus showed us another way. We don't *have* to be slaves to destruction any longer. Jesus taught us how to say yes to holiness (wholeness, goodness, maturity) and no to sin (bondage and idolatry).

The Bible tells us that we are slaves to whatever controls us (2 Peter 2:19). Ask yourself whether you have been captured by the cravings of your own heart. Have you been bowing down to the ranting and ravings of another person, or caving in to another's manipulations and demands, instead of listening for and obeying God's truth? Paul declares that we are no longer slaves to sin. We have been set free—our chains have been cut, the prison door unlocked, we are free to choose a new way of life (Romans 6:18; Galatians 5:1).

Right now you may not feel capable of making good choices for yourself. When you're in the habit of always giving in to your fears or to another person, you may indeed feel like you have no choices. You feel compelled to do what you've always done; what's familiar is easiest. You may want to change and make better choices but end up falling right back into destructive patterns of dependency, passivity, deceit, abuse, or controlling behaviors.

This may feel so unfamiliar and new that you don't know how to live this way, but give yourself some time. Put yourself among wise Christians who can help you learn how to think and choose differently. Start to ask yourself, "Does this choice I'm making right now lead me toward greater growth and maturity or more destruction?" As Moses encouraged the Israelites to do (Deuteronomy 30:19,20), choose life!

Take Responsibility to Define and Work on Your Problem

One of the most difficult things I teach my clients when they're in a destructive relationship is how to discern the difference between their problem and their partner's problem. In Debra's case, her problems included her anger, hurt, and insecurity, which were plenty difficult enough to work through. But instead of working on her own problems, Debra tried to own Sam's problem and made all sorts of attempts to "help" Sam conquer his sexual lust.

In my relationship with my mother, I spent time trying to get her to change. I wanted her to stop drinking, to get help, and to take her medication, all in the hopes that those remedies would help her to become a better mother and grandmother. Had she chosen to follow my recommendations, I'm sure they would have helped. But I had absolutely no control over my mother's choices, nor did I have any power to make her choose to stop drinking, get help, or take her medication. I didn't even have any influence over her. She was unwilling to hear me.

My mother's problems were not my problems or my fault, but

her problems contributed to my problems. I wanted a mother, and I didn't have the kind of mother I wanted. She had no desire to change. I became angry and resentful, hurt that she didn't care enough about her children to want to work on her issues. That became my problem, and I needed to figure out what I was going to do about my problem.

Eventually, if I wanted to be healthy, I had to acknowledge and then emotionally accept that my mother wasn't going to be the kind of mother I wanted. I had to forgive her and let my disappointment go. Was that difficult and painful? Of course it was, and as I mentioned earlier, my ability to do these things did not come quickly. But until I faced that reality and grieved my loss, I couldn't be free to move on with my life.

Drawing the Line

Debra's dilemma was that she didn't want to be with a man who preferred pornography over her. She found that hurtful and offensive (as any woman would). Yet instead of working on her pain, she tried to solve her husband's problem. It's true—solving Sam's trouble would have remedied Debra's as well, but she had no power to solve Sam's problem. Only Sam, with God's help, could tackle his own sin. Debra needed to work on her hurt, anger, ability to forgive, and the question of whether she could be with Sam if he chose not to work on his problem.

During one of my seminars, Loretta approached me to ask my advice on how she could help her husband handle his anger better. She said he wasn't really abusive; he was just under a lot of stress and had a rough childhood and easily lost control. When I asked Loretta what losing control meant, she said, "He doesn't hit me or anything like that, he just smashes things."

"What kind of things?" I asked her.

"Furniture, dishes, my knickknacks, the kids' toys," she replied, anxious to hear some ways that she might help him stop.

Instead I said, "Isn't it interesting, Loretta, that he never smashes or breaks his own things? Perhaps he has more control than you think. Why doesn't your husband get help or counseling for his anger problem or his childhood issues?" Sheepishly Loretta replied he didn't even know she was at the seminar.

"But since I'm here," Loretta continued, "what can *I* do? How do *I* help him?"

"Loretta, you're not clearly seeing what your problem is," I replied. "Your dilemma is not your husband's temper. That is his difficulty, and unfortunately you can't fix it for him. Only he can take responsibility for his temper and whatever hurts and frustrations he has from his past. However, you do have a problem. Your quandary is that you don't like living like this. You don't like living in fear of your husband's temper and walking on eggshells around the house. You don't like the example he's showing the children about how to handle stress and frustration. That is your problem. Now, how can I help you work on your problem?"

One of the reasons that we get so stuck in our destructive relationships is that we work on fixing the other person, which requires us to take responsibility for something we cannot control. You can't stop other people's destructive behavior. You can influence them and invite them to change (which we'll cover more in chapters 8 and 9) but you can't control or change them. All you can do is put an end to your part of the destructive cycle.

Take Responsibility for Your Own Unhealthy Patterns

Betty came to counseling because she said her mother was driving her crazy. Her father had divorced her mother ten years earlier, and from then on Betty's mom had leaned on her daughter for all her emotional support, transportation needs, spiritual encouragement, social life, and household responsibilities. The mother was in good health and perfectly capable of managing her own life, but she had always depended on her husband. Now that he was gone, she had transferred that dependency to her only daughter, Betty.

Betty felt trapped. She could never say no because of the guilt she would feel, but she grew to resent her mother and found herself responding to the incessant demands with sarcasm and frustration. Betty's harshness would cause her mother to withdraw for a bit, but not without first heaping guilt on Betty for failing to be a good daughter. Betty sincerely tried to be a good daughter, but she didn't know how to make her mother happy without killing herself. The problem for Betty was that she was attempting to manage the wrong life. She assumed responsibility for her mother's life but failed to take responsibility for her own. She was miserable and resentful and wanted to run away.

All relationships require either your willing or passive participation in order to survive. When you are a continuous victim, an unwilling and resentful martyr, or a participant in a string of destructive relationships, you must identify your part of the pattern in order to break free and become healthy. Instead, like Loretta and Betty, many of us attempt to remedy the relationship by taking responsibility for the other person's feelings or problems even if he or she doesn't admit to having a problem or doesn't really want to change.

Betty felt responsible for her mother's emotional well-being. Loretta felt responsible to manage her husband's temper and lack of self-control. Both were looking to fix or change the other person. It's not possible. Even if Betty's mother did want to become less dependent, or even if Loretta's husband wanted to manage his anger better, neither Loretta nor Betty can do the work to actually bring about the changes. Only the person with the problem can take responsibility for it. When we let others put the onus of their change on us, they make us responsible for them, which becomes a no-win proposition for all involved.

Recognizing and identifying our own destructive tendencies or immaturity empowers us to take back some control over our own life. Like Betty, do you allow others to become dependent upon you for their lives because their reliance makes you feel needed and important? Does resentment overtake you when you can't possibly meet their expectations? Or, like Betty's mother, are you looking for others to make you happy instead of making choices to enrich your own life? Perhaps you avoid conflict and fail to speak the truth when needed because you fear someone's disapproval and have put them in the god position in your life.

Do you permit yourself to be used and mistreated, yet keep believing the lie, as Loretta did, that there must be something you can do to change the other person? Do you know why you stay in the relationship when the other person won't stop hurting you? What needs to change in you so that you can become strong enough not to accept being terrorized in your own home or church or office?

It is essential that we take responsibility for our own thoughts, feelings, and actions. In doing this, please keep in mind that no one person can take total responsibility for the success of any relationship; that's a shared responsibility. Sometimes when we put a stop to our own destructive habits, our relationships actually get worse. If Betty stops catering to her mother's demands, tension will hum between them until Betty's mother decides whether she will pick up the reins of her own life. If Loretta speaks up, her husband may get angrier. We can choose to stop our own destructive patterns, but we cannot make a relationship healthy all by ourselves.

Take Responsibility to Get Healthier

You're beginning to identify your problem. You see the lies that you've believed, such as *I can't change,* or *I have no choices,* or *I must have* _____*'s love and approval in order to function,* or *It's all my fault, there's nothing I can do.* You're seeing the way you've tried to take responsibility to fix your partner's problem, used manipulation or anger to control someone, or allowed others to mistreat you or take advantage of you in order to feel loved or needed or to preserve the relationship. Now what?

Awareness is a good thing, but it's not enough to make change happen. We can be aware that we have a problem—we might need to lose weight or stop smoking or have a doctor check out that lump—but still not take action. If you want to stop the destruction in your life cycle, the next thing you have to do is make a decision. *What am I going to do differently? What small step can I make to change the way I think or the way I handle this destructive relationship I'm in? No one can change me but me, and it only begins when I decide.*

Let's say you, like millions of other people, want to lose weight. Can your friend or partner do that for you? Certainly they can support you or sabotage your efforts, but ultimately you have to take the responsibility for what food you are going to put into your mouth and whether you are going to exercise. No amount of pleading or nagging or loving or manipulating will actually take the weight off of your body. Even if your spouse made all the meals in such a way that eating them and nothing else would likely result in your losing weight, you can still choose to sneak off and eat forbidden foods. Only the person who owns the problem, decides to tackle the problem, and consistently makes the effort to confront the problem will successfully change. Your friends can't fix your problem, and you can't fix theirs.

Remember, when you try to make a change, your partner might not like it and might try to get you to return to your old ways. That's why it is so important for you to ask for third-party support to help and encourage you as you attempt to do things differently and become healthier.

ᕲ

In part 3, I will give you specific things you can do for yourself to begin growing and healing from a destructive relationship. First, though, the following three chapters show you three things you must decide to do if you want to stop your relationship from barreling on down the same destructive track:

1. Invite your partner to work with you to create a healthier relationship together. That requires you to learn to own your problem and *speak up* to your partner about how you feel and what you want to change.

2. If you're ignored, dismissed, mocked, manipulated, or emotionally battered, you will need to learn how and why to *stand up* to your partner.

3. You must be willing to *step back* from the relationship if necessary in order to stay safe and get healing. You will need to communicate clearly that you will no longer participate in the destructive dance if he or she will not change.

Let's start by learning how to invite healthy change by speaking up.

8

The Truth About Speaking Up: Your Voice Deserves to Be Heard

Any change, even a change for the better,
is always accompanied by drawbacks and discomforts.

ARNOLD BENNETT

Wise words bring many benefits,
and hard work brings rewards.

PROVERBS 12:14

A nn and Barb had been friends for nearly a year. They attended the same church, enjoyed small-group fellowship together, belonged to a women's Bible study, and spent a lot of time in each other's company. Ann would call Barb almost every day and talk nonstop about her difficult marriage, problems with her grown children, and the pressures and stress of life. Barb was a good listener and a good friend. Sometimes Ann would drop by Barb's house on her way somewhere, and they'd share a cup of tea and a few laughs or tears. Barb was always there for Ann, but Ann rarely asked Barb about her own life or difficulties.

Barb enjoyed Ann's company immensely, but she was getting a little worn out. Ann's problems overwhelmed Barb. She knew that she needed to have less drama and more space in her life for quiet solitude. She knew herself well enough to know that being busy and on the go all the time made her physically ill and emotionally vulnerable. Yet she never said anything to Ann when she dropped by unannounced or kept Barb on long phone calls. Barb didn't want to hurt Ann's feelings or upset their friendship. She didn't want Ann to feel unloved.

I share this example because it is so typical. We can all identify with Barb's dilemma. We start a new relationship and it feels great. Then over time, the friendship hits some snags, some awkwardness or difficulty. Yet we don't say anything. We don't express our feelings. The longer we wait, the more likely one of two things will happen: We will either get sick of keeping quiet (then emotionally explode all over our friend or distance ourselves from the relationship), or we will do nothing and become a martyr. Either way, we forfeit the blessings of a genuine mutual relationship.

When a relationship with someone lasts for any length of time, the involved parties form patterns, some healthy, others unhealthy. All relationships take on a shape. Once that shape has been established, changing it can be hard. For example, how difficult is it to speak to your parents about changing the traditional way of celebrating Christmas or Thanksgiving? Perhaps this year you'd like to do it at your house instead of packing up all the kids to take them to your parents' house, but you're too scared to approach them with this idea. They'd be hurt or offended. You don't want to risk hurting their feelings to suggest a change.

Or perhaps your house is the place where all the neighborhood kids play. At first it was wonderful—you could supervise what was happening and get to know your children's friends. But now some of your neighbors assume you're the resident babysitter. They run to the store or go to the doctor while their kids are with you, and they don't even tell you they're leaving. Your house is always a mess. Your fridge is empty and the noise is driving you crazy. How do you resign from being the neighborhood mom without feeling unac-commodating or unloving or selfish?

—◦—

Whenever we try to change the status quo of a relationship—better known as rocking the boat—we will face resistance (a little or a lot). We hate to do it because others may feel unhappy, uneasy, angry, or disappointed. They might attempt to stop us and return the relationship to the way it was. It's important to know up front that when we initiate a change, we will need to press through this awkward and uncomfortable stage until a new pattern is estab-lished that everyone can live with. Sometimes that never happens. Others might be unwilling to change or stop doing what is upset-ting. They might not want to compromise or negotiate to improve the relationship.

Even so, as we attempt to make new and healthier relation-ships (and discern potentially destructive ones), learning to *speak up* becomes essential. The longer we tolerate what is intolerable, the more difficult it will be to alter the relationship.

We cannot change or control another person, but as we mature, we can influence and invite them to change too.

Speaking Up

Many people find it impossible to speak up calmly and directly about what they don't like. Like Barb did with Ann, we put up and shut up because we don't want to upset anyone or have them think poorly of us—that is, until we're so angry we don't care anymore, and then we blow up. Then we feel guilty and ashamed and start the same dance all over again.

For us to grow and change, we must take responsibility for our-selves, understand our thoughts and feelings, face our fears, clarify in our own minds what our problem is, and gather our courage to speak up. God calls us to be *peacemakers,* not peacekeepers. As believers we are called to pursue peace, which may mean risking conflict in order to bring about a genuine peace (Psalm 34:14; Hebrews 12:14). It is not selfish to identify what you want or don't want and to share those things with others when appropriate. That kind of authenticity is an element of good mental and emotional health. We become selfish only when we are inconsiderate of what other people want or need, or when we expect everyone to cater to what we want all of the time.

Barb began to understand that she found it hard to honestly share with people what she wanted or needed from them. She felt guilty setting any kind of personal boundaries. This was a problem she carried with her from childhood, when she was never allowed to express her desires or feelings. It was not Ann's fault that Barb hadn't established some boundaries, but now the pattern had been set in which Ann felt perfectly free to stop by Barb's home without first checking out whether it was a good time for Barb. In addition, Barb felt hurt that Ann never asked about Barb's life or how Ann might pray for her. Barb realized that she had allowed Ann to become somewhat dependent on her as the strong, spiritual one. She understood that she had fostered that dependency by not opening up and mutually sharing with Ann her own weaknesses and struggles. These were Barb's problems, and she owned them.

As Barb reflected further, she realized that this pattern was rather typical of the way she related with other women. If she wanted to heal and grow, she would need to change. She always gave of herself to the point of exhaustion. Why was she afraid to say no? Barb feared rejection. She was afraid people wouldn't like her if she didn't give them what they wanted. And as she continued to reflect, she realized that she didn't like herself very much. No wonder it was hard for her to believe that others would like her. Yet Barb deeply wanted to be different and change the way she and Ann related. For the sake of their friendship, Barb realized she needed to initiate a conversation with Ann about her problems and their relationship.

When to Speak Up

If you are the kind of person who doesn't shy away from telling people what you think or how you feel about things, be careful not to speak without any reflection, prayer, or clear purpose. Venting to get something off your chest or tell someone off is never helpful to the other person, even if it makes you feel better for a time. The Bible warns us that "reckless words pierce like a sword" (Proverbs 12:18 NIV). Venting negative emotions without preparation can be very hurtful. Even speaking the truth to someone without having their good in mind can be destructive.

Before Barb approached Ann, she put a lot of thought and prayer into figuring out what she needed to say. If she had instead expressed anger in a moment of frustration and thoughtlessly said, "Why don't you ever call me before you just drop by?" or "You know, you never ask me about what's going on in my life. You're so self-centered," Ann would have rightly felt shocked, hurt, and confused. Barb never said these things bothered her before. Why now? Sometimes we create more problems because we don't put enough time into clarifying for ourselves what exactly we want to say.

In addition, speaking up for ourselves may feel a little selfish, because the Bible tells us to be patient with one another's faults (James 1:19; 1 Peter 4:8; 1 Thessalonians 5:14). We try not to make a big deal out of the problems. How can we know when we should continue to work on our patience or when we confront someone and speak up?

Often we need work on both areas. It's always good to give others grace and not bring up every little bothersome thing. But when someone deeply offends you or repeatedly does something that is hurtful, sinful, or destructive to you, to them, or to your relationship, God says to speak up, not be "tolerant." (See Leviticus 19:17, Matthew 18:15, and Luke 17:3 for some examples.)

Looking back, many individuals who have extricated themselves from destructive relationships said they saw the warning signs early in the relationship, but they didn't know what to do or weren't paying enough attention to their own feelings about the danger. Patty told me, "I was too afraid to speak up and risk a confrontation. I didn't want to offend or hurt her. I was trying so hard to be patient and long-suffering that I allowed myself to be walked on."

Nellie said, "I saw some warning signs, but I didn't heed them." She told me the story of a friendship that became like a scene from the movie *Fatal Attraction.* "I should have paid more attention and acted on my instincts earlier."

Listen to your instincts. They too will help you to know when you need to speak up.

How to Speak Up

When you plan to speak with someone who has sinned against you or hurt you, approach that person with humility (Galatians 6:1). You may be justifiably angry or hurt, but you must first do the work that prepares your heart to remove the log in your own eye before you can safely tackle the speck that is in his eye. Most people find it difficult to respond positively to another person's anger or constructive criticism, yet when you express your thoughts, feelings, and concerns with humility, your words are easier for the other person to take in (Psalm 141:5).

And that *is* the goal, isn't it? We want others to hear us, to care about our feelings, and to work with us to mend our relationship. We can't control how they will respond when we speak up, but we can make it more likely they will respond positively if we start our conversation with the right heart attitude.

Reading the signs. Barb told Ann she needed to speak with her about something important and asked her when it would be a good time for them to get together. Ann offered to come over right then. Barb gathered her courage and told Ann that it wasn't a good time for her (she'd never said no before), but Ann insisted she couldn't wait; she was coming right over.

Learn to pay attention. This was not a good sign. If you try to speak up even a little bit like Barb did when she told Ann, "No. Not now," and the other person runs right over you, you will have to make a choice right on the spot. Are you going to let this happen, or are you going to speak up again, this time in a stronger tone? Don't forget: When making a change in a relationship's established pattern, the other person will try to pull you back into the old rut. Stay strong and resolute.

One of the characteristics of a destructive relationship is a regular disregard of the felt needs, feelings, or concerns of the other person, and an attitude that says, *My feelings, needs, and desires always come first.* If you choose not to confront this attitude of entitlement, the other person's pattern of disregarding your feelings will continue.

It's impossible to know if Ann ignored Barb's feelings because she was fearful about what Barb planned to say and wanted to control the situation, or whether Ann was more selfish and didn't really think or care about Barb's feelings. Either way, Ann demonstrated she was not ruled by Christ or by his love in that moment. That's why it was imperative Barb not let this go. If others don't listen to you or respect your request, ask them why. Your speaking up gives them an opportunity right in the moment to observe their controlling behavior. This is not only good for you, it's good for them. You are seizing an opportunity to love them well (Ecclesiastes 7:5; James 5:19-20).

When Ann showed up at Barb's door, Barb was tempted to pretend she wasn't home. She wasn't ready to engage in a discussion with Ann, especially now that she felt cornered and angry that Ann disrespected her wishes. But Barb again ignored her own feelings and reluctantly answered the doorbell. Again she told Ann that she wasn't feeling well and that today was not a good time to talk.

Ann marched right in as if she never heard Barb and insisted that Barb tell her what was wrong right now.

It is important to notice how controlling Ann is being in this moment. She is insisting Barb do things her way. Barb stayed passive, choosing again not to speak up and confront Ann's controlling tactics. Instead of asking Ann to leave and to respect that this was not a good time, Barb became rattled and ended up saying some things she wished she hadn't. Instead of talking to Ann in the manner she'd originally planned, she ended up accusing Ann of being controlling and uncaring. Ann flew into a rage. She said she now knew what kind of person Barb really was, then walked out. Their friendship dissolved.

Learning the lesson. Devastated, Barb took responsibility for her failure to stand firm with Ann when Ann rushed over to talk. She realized that her new resolve surprised Ann; naturally, Ann was going to react against that. Barb also realized that Ann was not as good a friend as she first thought. She wouldn't listen to Barb, nor did she show concern for Barb's feelings. In spite of the deep pain Barb felt, she matured through the experience by learning more about herself and how to discern destructive people.

I share this story because as you learn to become healthier, you may find that your old friends don't like the new you. In the past you may have been drawn to people who are relationally or spiritually immature. You might be disappointed to discover that they are not as eager as you are to grow and to change. As you read once again the description from chapter 1 about what constitutes a healthy relationship, ask yourself, *Are my friendships mutual, respectful, caring, and honest?* Perhaps not as much as you'd like them to be. But when you begin to ask for those things, expect some people to feel surprised or even offended, saying, "What's wrong with you?"

Keep in mind as you change, you're changing your relational

dance pattern. As you do this, your dance partner will resist and try to get you to stop, often by stepping on your toes. Try not to get defensive, but stay firm. Continue to state the problem and what you'd like to see different.

SUCCESSFUL CONFRONTATION

When you need to confront someone, begin the process by speaking up about your feelings or desires or what has hurt you. Here are a few tips that may make this kind of conversation more successful:

1. Plan your words (Proverbs 15:28). Try to use language that doesn't attack the other person but rather states the problem with the other person's behavior or attitudes. For example, "I feel hurt that you're not hearing me right now, Ann," rather than, "You're not hearing anything I say," or, "You never listen."

2. Seek a mutually good time (Proverbs 29:20). Make sure you choose a time when both of you are rested and have the time to discuss the problem. When people are exhausted or distracted, it is more likely that they will resort to habitual patterns that are unhealthy or destructive.

3. Watch your body language and voice tone. This is very important. Approaching someone with humility doesn't mean you should use a weak voice tone. At this level of confrontation, it is best to remain neutral in body language and tone, like you were asking someone to pass the salt and pepper at dinner. It's best to be clear, firm, and gracious, not tentative, unsure, or emotionally volatile.

4. Listen to another perspective if the other person offers one. Allow the other person to share personal feelings or desires, but don't get sidetracked. Don't debate feelings or be talked out of your concerns. Restate them one more time.

Examples of Speak-up Dialogues

Learning to speak up takes practice and patience with yourself, and sensitivity to the uniquenesses of the particular situation. The following examples might help you to begin thinking about how you can best speak up.

1. Here's what Barb might have said initially to Ann when she showed up at her door.

> *Ann, as I said on the phone, this isn't a good time. I really don't feel well today and don't have the energy to talk in a constructive way. Can we do this tomorrow or whenever it is best for both of us?*

If Ann still refuses, Barb will need to state the same thing but more firmly.

> *Ann, I said I'm not feeling well. This is not a good time for me. I can't talk right now.*

Once Barb is rested and they plan a time to talk, here is a sample of what Barb could say to Ann to invite her into a healthier, more mutual relationship.

> *Thanks, Ann, for coming. I appreciate it. I so value our friendship. You've been a lot of fun for me and I enjoy spending time with you. But I have a problem. Actually I've had it for a long time, but I just never told you about it and I need to. I tire easily and don't have as much stamina as you seem to have. I need to take a lot of time out to rest and be quiet in order to function. I would appreciate it if you'd call me ahead of time the next time you'd like to stop by. Sometimes your visits don't come at a good time for me, and I haven't been completely honest. I also can't continue our long phone conversations at night. How about I call you at night if I'm feeling up for it?*

Barb should stop here and wait for Ann's response. If it is positive and Ann is hearing Barb, then Barb can continue.

> *I'd like our friendship to deepen, and so I want you to understand some of my struggles. My health is one of them. Would you be willing to pray for me?*

Again Barb should wait for Ann's response. Barb is inviting Ann to care for her and is changing some of their old patterns. If Ann gets defensive or blaming, Barb must not engage in a debate over the validity of her requests, nor argue with Ann. She should simply restate her need:

> *Ann, I want our friendship to continue, but in order for it to do so in a way that's good for me, I have to be honest with you about my limits.*

Ann may need some time to think about Barb's request because Barb is changing things between the two of them. When you make such changes, it's important to give the other person some space to think it over, but if he or she continues to repeat the old patterns, disregarding what you have said, you will need to move to the next step of inviting healthy change, which is to stand up.

Before we talk about how to do that, let's take another look at some of the previous examples of destructive relationships and speak-up dialogues that might invite healthy change.

2. Here's how Terri might speak up to John about his attempts to teach her what is best (see chapter 1).

> *John, we need to talk. I've realized something about our relationship that's taken me a long time to figure out. It feels to me like you are trying to change me into the person you think I should be. I have a problem with that. I want to be my own person with my own thoughts and ideas and feelings. I'm not*

*the same as you are, and I don't always want the same things
you do. When you try to convince me I'm wrong or make fun
of the way I do things, you disrespect and demean me, and I
don't like it one bit. It hurts and I'd like you to stop.*

Terri should stop talking and wait for John's response. He probably will become defensive or blame Terri. For example he might
say, "I'm not doing anything wrong. You're just too sensitive. Get
over it."

It's Terri's turn to show John exactly what he does. She should
speak up again and say,

*John, right now you're disrespecting and demeaning me again.
You're telling me I'm too sensitive just because I'm not like
you. I am sensitive, and I've tried for years to pretend that
your insults don't bother me, but they do. I'd like you to stop
treating me like I'm less just because I'm not like you. I like
the fact that I'm a sensitive person.*

If John refuses or continues mocking her, then Terri's next step
will be to stand up.

3. Here's an example of what Rita could have said to her parents, who
regularly interfered with her marriage (see chapter 1).

*Mom and Dad, I love you and I know you only want the best
for me. But I'm a grown woman who is married, and I have
a problem acting that way when you always tell me what to
do. I don't want to disrespect you, but it's time you let go and
let me live my own life. I want to make my own decisions
with my new husband. If I want your opinion or advice, I'll
ask for it. I do value your perspective, but for now, I want
you to stop interfering and let me try to think for myself. Will
you do that?*

Rita should stop here and allow them a chance to respond. If

Rita's parents agree to respect her wishes, she shouldn't expect instant change. When we ask for a change, quite often people will agree to do what we ask but then quickly fall back into their previous patterns. When that happens, simply remind them of your new resolve and their commitment to change. Rita's parents agreed to back off, but the next day they were again telling Rita what to do.

> *Mom, remember our conversation from yesterday? I told you I needed to learn to make my own decisions. If I want your and Dad's advice, I'll ask you for it. But for now, I'd like you to let me make my own decision as you previously agreed to do.*

Rita might need to say this over and over again to whatever reasons they come up with for breaking their commitment. Her parents might argue, *But Rita, we just thought...But Rita, we think you're making a terrible mistake...*

If Rita backs down now and allows her parents to interfere again, she resumes the old dance. She must keep restating her desire for change. If they continue to interfere and criticize her decisions even though they said they would stop, Rita will need to stand up.

4. *Phil and Joanne were disappointed and unhappy with each other* and justified their explosive anger and disrespectful comments (see chapter 1). Here's how Phil might have initiated a healthy change.

> *I'm aware that I have not treated you very well lately. I've justified my meanness because of my hurt and disappointment in our relationship. But I do not like the person I'm becoming, and I also don't think God's very pleased with my heart right now. I want to grow and figure out a way to get along with you so that our marriage can be better for both of us. I know you're not happy and I'm not happy either. I'm not sure what we can do next, but right now I'm willing to work on treating*

you with more respect and stop calling you names. Would you be willing to do that as well?

GET SAFE AND STAY SAFE

It is empowering to learn to speak up, but be careful. If you are being physically abused, or if you feel threatened even if you've never been touched, speaking up may result in more abuse (Proverbs 13:1). In addition to learning how to speak up, it may be time for you to make a plan to get safe and stay safe, period. Trust me: In cases of regular verbal, physical, or sexual abuse, your spouse cannot be talked into changing his or her ways. Nothing short of drastic action will wake him or her up. Please consult with a woman's shelter or an abuse counselor with expertise in physically abusive relationships. It is beyond the scope of this book to wisely advise someone how to make a detailed safety plan that includes children. (See endnote 1 for helpful resources as well as "Resources for Further Help" at the end of the book.)

Phil should stop here and wait for Joanne's response. In part, she will be watching him to see if his resolve is sincere. When Phil falls back to his old behavior, he must own it, confess it, and ask for forgiveness. That will demonstrate that he is taking responsibility for his part of the change and prove his commitment to the process. If Joanne agrees with Phil to work together on being more respectful of each other and she backslides, he should wait for her to ask for his forgiveness. If she fails or refuses, he can remind her of her commitment to change and see what happens. If she is not willing to work on her part of their destructive dance, Phil should continue to work on his part but may need to move to the next level by standing up.

5. Loretta wanted to know how to help her husband's temper problem (see chapter 7). Once we clarified what Loretta's problem was, she could speak up. If you are in an emotionally abusive relationship or are living with someone who has an explosive temper (but no physical abuse), your initial speak-up dialogue will very likely fall on deaf ears.

Here's an example of what Loretta might say to her angry husband.

> *Sam, I love you and I want our relationship to work. You have many good qualities. You work hard, you are handy around the house, and I like your sense of humor, but there is something happening that is terribly upsetting to me. When you get angry, you lose control of yourself. You break things, smash my dishes, throw the kids' toys, and scare us all to death. I can't fix your problem for you. I know you're hurting from some things in your past and the stress at work, but I don't want to live like this anymore. I feel like I'm always walking on eggshells around you. It's stressful and unhealthy for me and the children. But it's also unhealthy for you. I'd like you to get help for your problem.*

The likely response Loretta will get is more anger or sulking self-blame that doesn't actually lead to any change. That doesn't mean she shouldn't say what she needs to say. However, Sam will probably attempt to get Loretta to back down by frightening her with his anger, or making her feel pity for him, which is his typical way to control Loretta.

She can't control Sam's temper, but Loretta can stop allowing his moods to control her. Anyone involved in an emotionally abusive relationship, as well as those involved in other forms of destructive relationships, will often have to move to the next step, which is to stand up.

⁓

In summary, to speak up effectively, follow these steps:

- *Pray*
- *Prepare*
- *Practice*

- *Plan the time*
- *Persevere*

Start by praying. Ask God for the wisdom to speak the truth in love. Next prepare what you want to say and how you want to say it. Practice out loud as many times as necessary in order to feel like you can say what you need to the way you want to say it. Plan the time and place; make sure you're safe when you say it.

Changing ourselves is difficult. Changing the dynamics of a relationship is even harder. Persevere. Don't give up. Keep speaking. Even if you don't receive a positive response from your partner, remind yourself that by changing your part, you are growing and becoming healthier and more mature. Then, if it's necessary, learn how to stand up.

The Truth About Standing Up:
You Can Become a Champion of Peace

People may not like it, and often they won't understand,
but with grace it is possible to be strong without being mean.

GERALD MAY, MD

A man who remains stiff-necked after many rebukes
will suddenly be destroyed—without remedy.

PROVERBS 29:1 NIV

W hen talking with clients about what they need to do to stop the destructiveness in their relationships, I often use this illustration. I scoot my office chair close to where they're sitting and start to gently kick them in the shins. They look at me wide-eyed, surprised by my unusual behavior, but usually they just sit there, allowing me to continue kicking them.

I say, "Now what are you supposed to do?" They sit passively, not exactly sure. I tell them, "It's time to speak up. Say *Ouch* or *Stop* or *Don't do that, I don't like that.*"

Then they laugh and say, "Okay—stop, I don't like that. It hurts me."

But they're not very convincing, so I ignore them, or laugh at them and continue to swing my foot into their shins. They usually say it again, this time a little firmer, but I continue to kick them. I change the subject or tell them they're too sensitive, that they're making a big deal out of nothing. I might say my behavior is their fault, because they aggravated me, or I might claim that I can't help it, this is just what counselors do when they're frustrated. By now their legs are more than a little sore.

"What's your response to my indifference? Or my excuses?" I ask. "What are you going to do about your problem?"

Many are tempted at this point to argue with me about my excuses or rationalizations or justifications for kicking them. Some even try to understand why I feel the way I do. "Don't do it!" I tell them. "You'll get sidetracked. Your problem is that I'm not stopping when you asked me and that I'm not respecting you right now. Period! What are you going to do about it?"

Eventually they get it. They stand up and in a firm voice say, "Stop kicking me! If you don't stop right now then I will have to leave." I stop. I realize they mean business. They aren't going to tolerate my inappropriate behavior. This is what I'm after. They can't stop me from kicking them or thwart me from justifying it or blaming them, but they can block my leg from hitting theirs by moving back from me and informing me of the consequences if I don't stop.

Why Stand Up?

As silly as this illustration is, people get the point. Your passivity is detrimental when others lie to you, ignore you, treat you disrespectfully, or use you. Getting caught up in defending your request that someone stop their hurtful behavior is also counterproductive. When you stand up, don't see the action as merely standing up for yourself. For many of us that feels too self-centered, and at times it might be.

When we stand up to a destructive person, we are standing up for something bigger than just our own feelings. We are standing up *for* goodness, truth, righteousness, and peace. In addition, as

Jesus always did, we are standing up *against* sin, evil, wickedness, lawlessness, and abuse of power and privilege. We need make no apologies for standing up when we need to. Jesus never did.

Whenever Christ spoke to people about their obvious wrong behaviors or deceptively sinful hearts, anyone who humbly acknowledged his or her failings received nothing but gracious, tender compassion from him. Those who refused to listen or acknowledge their wrongdoing received a more potent dose of truth—not because Jesus loved them less, but like strong ammonia revives the faint, hard truth can shock us into awareness. (See, for example, Matthew 23 or Mark 7:6-13.)

All people are precious to God (including you). He has created you in his image with dignity and value and purpose. You may not feel this way about yourself yet, but it's true. God loves you and not only wants to teach you how to love others well, he wants to help you take a stand against sin. You are not someone else's property or an object to be used or abused; don't allow yourself to be treated as such. Submitting to mistreatment is destructive to you and to those who treat you in such a devaluing way. They not only diminish your personhood, they diminish their own. This is not what people were made for.

When you continue to offer yourself in relationship to people who consistently mistreat you, disrespect you, control you, abuse you, deceive you, and use you, you will feel sicker and sicker (Proverbs 4:14-27). Jesus tells us in Matthew 18 that when people are blind to their sin against you, we are to enlist others to help them see. This step is part of standing up. You take a stand with a supportive person or community by your side and together declare, "My requests are not negotiable. I will not continue to live in fear," or "be controlled," "be disrespected," "be degraded," "be lied to," or "be ignored" as it is appropriate to your situation.

When you finally stand up, don't be surprised if you find yourself being accused of non-Christian, mean, abusive, and controlling behavior. The other person will likely retaliate against your newfound strength and want you to back down by trying to make you feel afraid or guilty. He or she may accuse you of being too sensitive, too selfish, or unrealistic in your expectations. The implication is that you have no right to challenge the way he or she treats you.

That is not true. God calls us to treat others with love, grace, kindness, and truth. Stay calm but firm. If you back down now, you will continue in the destructive dance. If you are being consistently mistreated or hurt in your relationship, it is imperative for the health of your relationship as well as for your own mental, emotional, and spiritual well-being that you stand up and stay standing (Proverbs 25:26).

Standing up for truth and righteousness, against sin, with others by our side helps us stand firm. Ideally, the other person will accept responsibility to change his or her destructive ways. If not, the next step is to distance ourselves from the relationship, sometimes temporarily, sometimes permanently.

Step Back

Conflict is inevitable in any relationship. Yet when a participant will not see or take responsibility for serious sin against us after we have spoken up and stood up, the only thing left for us to do is to step back.

Jesus says, "If he refuses to listen even to the church, treat him as you would a pagan or a tax collector" (Matthew 18:17 NIV). Jesus is saying that when someone refuses to hear our concerns, our relationships change. The people of Jesus' day didn't trust pagans and tax collectors. These individuals were never part of a Jewish person's inner circle of friends. A good Jew might help a tax collector or pagan if there was a need, and certainly he would be respectful toward them, but he would never intimately fellowship with them.

Being in a close relationship with someone is not a right, even if both people are Christians. It is a sacred privilege. The apostle

Paul advises us to distance ourselves from people who are continually destructive, especially if they claim to be Christian, in order to send a clear message that their behaviors or attitudes are sinful and unacceptable, both to us and to God (1 Corinthians 5, especially verse 11). Stepping back when necessary helps minimize the damage that the destructive person inflicts on us and our children.

Creating Separation

Not everyone is able to physically distance themselves from someone who is destructive. But creating separation can be very helpful, even if you only do it temporarily.

Francine was married to a man who said he was a Christian. He had a hot temper and poor self-control. Frank never touched Francine with his hands, but his harsh words wounded her spirit more than any punch could have. He used verbal weapons to attack Francine whenever she didn't cooperate with his agenda, made a mistake, or did something he thought was stupid. Francine tried speaking up and sharing how his outbursts hurt her. Frank heard her, and sometimes he even seemed genuinely sorry, but he didn't change his behavior.

Next Francine tried standing up. One evening as Frank was in the midst of an outburst she firmly said, "Stop it right now!" Startled, Frank chuckled at his wife's newfound assertiveness and continued his tirade, although it didn't last as long.

Finally Francine decided to step back. Frank's words cut her to the core, and she felt like she was being punched again and again. She was no longer going to allow that to happen. Because he wouldn't control himself and she couldn't control him, she chose to leave and not allow herself to be treated in that way. Together we made a plan so that next time Frank began to get riled up, Francine would be prepared.

Francine decided that she would leave their home the minute

Frank got started. She knew his patterns long enough to know what was coming. She would grab her purse and walk right out the door. (They had no children, who should be included in any exit plan.) Francine made an extra set of car keys, which she put in the garage. She hid some cash there as well, just in case she had to leave without her purse. In her trunk she packed an overnight bag and a coat, so that she would not need to come home until the next day.

The next time Frank began to lose control, Francine implemented her plan. Frank found he had no one to yell at but the four walls. Later, Francine called him from her cell phone. She said, "I'm not going to allow myself to be your verbal punching bag anymore. The way you talk to me is hurtful and disrespectful. You dishonor me as your wife and as God's daughter. When you act that way you also degrade yourself. I still love you and I will be home tomorrow after work. This will give you some time to get control over your temper and think about things."

Francine continued to implement her plan whenever Frank started to demean and disrespect her. He soon learned that it was expensive for him to lose control of himself as the credit card bills for her hotel began to mount.

Stepping back was good for both Francine and Frank. Francine saved herself from bearing the brunt of Frank's emotional dumping and ill-will during its greatest intensity. She did not have his ugly words to ponder throughout the night, nor did she have to struggle with forgiving him for hurting her. She also realized that she did not have to feel guilty for leaving, because she was actually helping him to learn how to control himself. She saw that her choices were good for both of them.

Frank finally understood Francine was not going to tolerate his abusive behavior anymore, and he began to learn how to handle his anger and disappointment in different, healthier ways. He always knew it was wrong to treat Francine the way he did, but now that he had to experience painful consequences (financial and relational), he took his problem more seriously.

If you are unable to physically distance yourself from a relationship, learn how to emotionally distance yourself so that you continue to get healthier and the other person realizes that you mean what you say. People who are destructive should lose the privilege of your fellowship. That does not mean that you have to turn your back on the person in question. Step back while still facing forward, inviting that person to change so that reconciliation may be possible.

Why Step Back?

I said in the introduction to this book that for a 15-year period I did not see my mother, and now I'm going to explain why. After losing custody of her children, my mother chose not to remain closely involved in our lives. I too made the choice to distance myself from my mother and sent only the obligatory cards at Christmas and Mother's Day. (Someone needs to make Mother's Day cards for those who have destructive relationships with their mothers.) Let me share a little more of my own experience in this relationship.

To Gain Time to Heal

Even though I was a Christian and a brand-new counselor, I was not emotionally or spiritually strong enough to know how to be in my mother's presence without getting demoralized as well as furious by her hurtful words. Even sporadic contact with her resulted in anger, introspective self-blame, and self-pity. My thoughts ran like this: *What did I do to make my mother hate me so much? Why doesn't she see any good in me? How can I get her to see and admit her destructiveness toward me and get her to be sorry for it?*

Over the years I tried speaking up. I got nowhere. I also stood up and told her firmly what she was doing that hurt me. It didn't matter. She denied it. She blamed me. She exhibited no repentance, no awareness, and no desire to change. Finally I stepped back, not only from trying to get her to be different toward me, but from all personal contact. I needed to heal, and I needed to learn how to be near someone who was destructive without allowing her to devastate me. That took time. There is no such thing as instant healing or painless maturity.

Like me, you may need to step back to give yourself time to heal and grow. You might believe that nothing is changing, there is no hope of anything changing, and you can't continue to live the way you have been. Emotionally you're drained, mentally you're confused, spiritually you feel dry or disconnected, and you need to get some fresh air.

A destructive relationship can be a lot like a toxic environment. Depending upon how toxic it is, things die within its boundaries. It might be your relationship that dies. It might be your faith. It might even be your sense of self. Don't let that happen if you can help it. No one in his right mind would continue to live in a toxic environment without either trying to change it, open windows for fresh air, put on a protective suit, or get out. Who can expect anyone to thrive in this kind of environment? It's not possible.

Whether you step back temporarily or more permanently, use this time wisely. If you're stepping back from your marriage or other personal relationship, now is not the time to rush into another relationship. If you do this, you will probably repeat the same destructiveness that you just escaped. Now is the time for you to stop, take responsibility for your own areas of sin and immaturity, start healing, learn how to establish healthier relationships and boundaries, and deepen your intimacy with God. During this time apart, remember to pray for the other person, so that he or she might start to wake up and begin to grow too.

You might be surprised to learn that God does not require us to open ourselves up to everyone. Jesus didn't (John 2:23-25). He also advises us to stay away from certain kinds of people precisely because they are destructive. (See, for example, Proverbs 1:15; 14:7; 21:28; 22:24; 1 Corinthians 15:33.) God commands us to love everyone, including our enemies, but that doesn't mean we must have close fellowship with them. In fact, we can't. That's precisely why they're called enemies.

To Give the Gift of Consequences

Francine's purpose in stepping back from Frank was different than mine was with my mother. She was hoping to communicate in the strongest way possible (short of permanent separation) that she was not going to continue the same old dance with Frank. If he wouldn't change, she would!

When you communicate your boundaries to someone, it's important to state them correctly. Otherwise you will get stuck trying to get someone to do something you have no control over. For example, Francine correctly said to Frank, "I will not allow myself to be treated this way any longer."

Francine had control over what she allowed herself to do or not do, but she had no control over Frank. If she had said, "I will not allow you to treat me this way any more," her announcement would have less of an impact, because she can't control Frank. The only time the "I will not allow you" kind of statement works is when we really have power over someone and can enforce our expectations, such as parents can with their child or a boss can with an employee or an abuser can with his victim.

Stepping back can be especially effective when the other person wants the relationship to continue. If the person doesn't care, the action has less impact.

If the destructive partner is a spouse, implementing a more permanent separation from him or her becomes complicated because of finances, children, as well as the Bible's teaching about marriage and divorce. If your efforts to take the other steps have yielded no changes, it's time to involve your pastor and specific church leaders so that you are supported if you decide to take this next step (see Matthew 18:15-20).

Jesus calls us to be peacemakers instead of peacekeepers, who pretend all is well in order to maintain an illusion of peace. Terri tried that for years with John (chapter 1), and her passivity almost ended up destroying her and their marriage. Seeking genuine peace between two individuals may require tough action, especially when one party continues to be blind, unresponsive, or unrepentant. As a Christian counselor, I do not advise marital separation lightly; however, in some cases it is the only way to obtain the necessary space to think clearly, pray, and heal, as well as to communicate to the destructive partner in the strongest possible way that the relationship will not continue without change.

CONSEQUENCES—A GIFT?

In my book *How to Act Right When Your Spouse Acts Wrong,* I talk about giving the gift of consequences to help someone wake up to his or her own blindness and destructive behavior. Painful consequences are one of God's most powerful ways to teach us to stop sinning and to live well (see Galatians 6:7). Recently I had the sad task of helping parents implement some painful consequences for their adult daughter, who was abusing cocaine and destroying her life. They didn't do these things to harm their daughter but to help her wake up so that she would take responsibility for her problem and change.

Paul encourages us to distance ourselves from other believers who are sinning and refuse correction. (See for example, 1 Corinthians 5:9-11; 2 Thessalonians 3:6,14-15.) If the circumstances of your relationship are not changing in spite of everything else you have done thus far, it may be time for you to consider separating for the purpose of genuine reconciliation (2 Corinthians 7:10).

"As far as it depends on you," Paul says, "live at peace with everyone" (Romans 12:18 NIV). Biblical peace doesn't merely imply an absence of conflict between people but a genuine state of harmony, communion, and unity.[1] Paul tells us to "make every effort to do what leads to peace and to mutual edification" (Romans 14:19 NIV). As Christians, we are to take the initiative to bring healing and restoration to our relationships, all the while knowing that the results aren't totally up to us.

To Wait in Love

In the meantime, what do we do, and for how long?

There is plenty to do to heal and grow while stepping back from a destructive person. Much of it we will cover in chapters 10 through 12. Waiting on God and waiting on someone else is hard work. We want action and look for immediate results, and when we don't see them coming anytime soon, we can become discouraged and tempted to give up.

While God's Word does not require us to stay in relationship with everyone, we are more committed to certain people, either through blood or marriage, and these people might be the very ones who are most destructive in our lives (Micah 7:6). We hope for them to change or come to their senses, and our expectations rise when we think that perhaps they're starting to wake up, but how can we tell if we're witnessing genuine change or merely lip service?

What Is Genuine Repentance?

Only God can judge a person's heart, but the Bible does tell us how to discern whether repentance is genuine. Feeling sad or shedding profuse tears, however, are not signs. Many of us get hooked back into a destructive relationship by a person's strong emotions. They cry, they plead, they tell us how much they love us. They beg for another chance and become sweet and kind and wonderful, and before long we're back with them, swept right down the same path of more destruction. Tears indeed are the language of the heart but what exactly are their tears saying? *I'm so sorry. I've sinned against God and you,* or *Poor me, I feel devastated because you left me,* or *because you put these consequences in place.* There is a huge difference.

The apostle Paul wrote a tough letter to the Corinthians, rebuking them about some serious wrongs. They felt sad and hurt. But Paul distinguished between two kinds of sorrow. One is a godly remorse over one's sin against God and against another person. The other kind of sorrow is our emotional pain over the consequences we have to pay when we sin. This "worldly sorrow," as Paul calls it, is more self-oriented than God-oriented (2 Corinthians 7:8-12).

If you're looking for repentance, listen carefully to what others say when they are emotional. Are they aware of the pain they have caused? Do they show concern for your suffering? Do they acknowledge their deeper heart issues, such as selfishness, laziness, or pride? What happens when you won't fellowship with them immediately and ask them to go to weekly counseling on their own for a period of time? Are they willing to do whatever it takes to change, even without promises of reconciliation or relationship? If not, then their sadness is sorrow for themselves, not godly sorrow. You will not know whether the things they promise you are true without giving it plenty of time. Words won't show you these things, only actions over time will (Matthew 7:20; 1 Corinthians 4:20).

Can a destructive person change? Yes. However, the apostle Paul warns us not to be fooled or fool ourselves. When we change, we do not continue in those same sinful behaviors. He writes,

> Those who indulge in sexual sin, or who worship idols, or commit adultery, or are male prostitutes, or practice homosexuality, or are thieves, or greedy people, or drunkards, or are abusive, or cheat people—none of these will inherit the Kingdom of God. *Some of you were once like that.* But you were cleansed; you were made holy; you were made right with God by calling on the name of the Lord Jesus Christ and by the Spirit of our God (1 Corinthians 6:9-10).

In my experience, when destructive people finally come to counseling or are willing to admit they have a problem, they often do this in order to get the other person to back down from the new boundaries or consequences, not because they own what needs to change in them. They may have some superficial awareness they need healing, but they want it on their terms.

Testing the Response

In the Old Testament, Naaman angrily refused the prophet Elisha's treatment plan for his leprosy. He wanted his healing to be easy, quick, and painless. *Why should I have to go and wash myself seven times in the filthy Jordan River? Why couldn't Elisha just wave his hands over me, or say a prayer?* Elisha didn't back down, and Naaman wisely realized that if he wanted to be healed, he would need to submit himself to what the prophet said to do (2 Kings 5:1-15).

Pay attention. Is the destructive person in your life willing to submit to church discipline and counseling to get help for her problem? Is she willing to work until she consistently demonstrates a changed heart as well as changed behaviors? You will only know the answers when you patiently wait in love. Once you've separated yourself from the person, full reconciliation should not occur until you and others observe consistent (not perfect) changes over a period of time.

Joseph used this same process to test his brothers. He had no contact with them for years after they sold him into slavery. When they came to him for food during a famine in their own country, they had no idea that the person they were talking with was their brother Joseph, though he knew who they were. Although Joseph was gracious, even generous, to his brothers, he did not trust them. He remembered their treachery and did not make himself vulnerable to them. In fact, he put them through a series of tests to expose what was going on in their hearts. On the surface they looked like changed men. But what was really going on? Were they still selfish or envious of their youngest brother, Benjamin, like they had been with Joseph? Would they trade Benjamin to save their own skins? It was only after much time and testing that Joseph let down his guard and invited his brothers back into his life. (See Genesis 37–45 for the complete story.)

Test the other person. See how he responds to you when you don't give him what he wants. If you don't see consistent changes in the way he thinks, acts, and interacts with you and others, don't for a minute believe his words or his profuse tears (Proverbs 26:23-24). Jesus said, "Produce fruit in keeping with repentance" (Matthew 3:8 NIV).

A WORD ABOUT BIBLICAL LOVE

Many of the steps outlined in this chapter are extremely difficult for most of us to take because they make us feel mean and uncaring. It doesn't help that destructive people will tell us we're being hurtful or controlling when we stand up or step back. Therefore, I think it's essential we get clear-headed about godly love.

Paul says that godly love does no harm (Romans 13:10). That does not mean that biblical love never hurts. Jesus often spoke sternly to the Pharisees, and Proverbs reminds us that a good friend might inflict loving wounds (Proverbs 27:6). All of us find it painful to swallow the medicine of hard truth. It hurts, but it heals.

Biblical love involves self-sacrifice and at times suffering, but let's understand the sacrifice that God asks us to make. When Jesus says, "Greater love has no one than this, that he lay down his life for his friends" (John 15:13 NIV), he is speaking of those who are willing to give up their lives (physically or otherwise) for the good or well-being of another.

Risking our lives and suffering third-degree burns, for example, in order to rescue a person from a burning building, is godly and sacrificial love. Living in a dangerous inner city in order to bring people to Christ demonstrates sacrificial love. But allowing someone to continually sin against us without protest or consequence isn't biblical love, it's foolishness. It is never in anyone's long-term best interest to allow them to keep sinning. Contrary to what destructive people will say, the most loving thing we could do for them is to hold them accountable for their actions. This indeed may cost us sacrifice and suffering. We do this not only for our benefit, but with the hope that as we draw a line in the sand and say "no more," they will wake up to their own sinfulness and repent.

Too many individuals have been wrongly instructed that biblical love means they must be nice and suffer quietly, even as they are mistreated and abused. But as C.S. Lewis wisely wrote, "Love is more stern and splendid than mere kindness."[2]

Part Three

Surviving It

God Sees You and Wants to Heal You

Although the world is full of suffering,
it is also full of overcoming it.

HELEN KELLER

The LORD is close to the brokenhearted;
he rescues those whose spirits are crushed.

PSALM 34:18

Depending on the kind of destructive relationship you have experienced and for how long, you may need healing in many different aspects of your life. Foundational to everything else, however, is healing in these two areas: your picture of God and your view of yourself.

How We See God

Once I asked one of my clients, Amy, about her picture of God. She told me, "When I was a child, my father would tell us a story about a gentleman who saw someone on a park bench grabbing pigeons and breaking their wings. When the gentleman asked the other man why he was doing such a cruel thing, he said he was trying to teach the pigeons that life is not a bed of roses." Amy's father told her this story to be funny, but Amy never laughed, and she likened the wing breaker's behavior to God's hand in her life. "He breaks people's wings in order to teach them something," she said. From her perspective, God seemed as cruel and unsympathetic as the man on the park bench.

Her story horrified and saddened me. God never inflicts needless pain or breaks our wings. Because of sin, we are already damaged, and we are living in a broken-down world. Pain and suffering are a consequence of this reality. God's message is clear: He longs to heal us and restore us to wholeness, not destroy us. In chapter 2, I briefly introduced you to the truth that we can know what God is like by looking at Jesus. The heart of the gospel message is that Jesus came to seek and to save lost people (Luke 19:10).

The Lost Find a Helper

Who are the lost? We all are. In the original language, the Greek word for *lost* means much more than being disoriented or unable to find one's way. To be *lost* means to be ruined or destroyed, whether physically or morally.[1] To be lost in any way is to be desperate. Let me now restate why God sent Jesus to earth: Jesus came to seek and save ruined, destroyed, desperate, disoriented people. Let's look at one of my favorite stories that illustrates so well God's tender heart for broken people.

> One Sabbath day as Jesus was teaching in a synagogue, he saw a woman who had been crippled by an evil spirit. She had been bent double for eighteen years and was unable to stand up straight. When Jesus saw her, he called her over and said, "Dear woman, you are healed of your sickness!" Then he touched her, and instantly she could stand straight. How she praised God! (Luke 13:10-13).

This woman, crippled by an evil spirit, suffered for a very long time. Perhaps you feel disfigured and stooped like this woman, even if your affliction is not physical, but emotional or spiritual or mental. You hurt so bad you can't stand straight anymore. Someone has injured you, broken your wings (or your spirit), but it wasn't God. Watch what Jesus does in this story.

First, he seeks out this woman. He sees her. She is one among many in the synagogue, but he notices her and her affliction. Though the passage doesn't tell us, I'm sure she saw Jesus too. But she held back and didn't go running to Jesus as many who wanted him to heal them did. Jesus called her over to him. Listen to how he addressed her. He said, "Dear woman." Jesus' heart broke to see her condition.

Do you know that you are just as important to God as this woman was? He sees your pain. He knows exactly where you are bent and unable to stand straight. He calls you to come to him, and he says you are dear to him.

Jesus healed her, and instantaneously she stood straight. Was life pain-free for her from then on? I doubt it. Let's use our imaginations for a moment to see how this woman's miraculous healing might have caused her some new pain and difficulty. First of all, the Pharisees were not happy with what Jesus did. Perhaps this woman encountered some rejection from her primary support group after Jesus left, because they disapproved of his healing on the Sabbath. She might also have suffered some economic repercussions, because now that she was healed, she was no longer eligible for financial help from the synagogue treasury. She would need to work or find a means of support, which she hadn't been able to do for 18 years. She might also encounter some interpersonal difficulties, because, instead of always staring at the floor bent in half like she was, she would now face people and look into their eyes. How might that change her relationship with them?

Although she rejoiced at her immediate physical healing, the process of healing her heart had only just begun. We don't know what difficulties she encountered later. Likewise, our healing and restoration, by which we become the people God designed us to be, may involve additional suffering or pain. When God allows it, please trust him; pain and suffering are always part of our healing, not our breaking. A doctor may cause pain when resetting a broken limb, and a physical therapist's exercises may be agonizing after surgery, but these are critical to recovery. God knows that pain is a necessary part of growth and healing. Just as in the story of the bent woman, healing often brings about drastic changes in our life. It is impossible to navigate all of those changes without some pain.

Will You Believe Him?

I wonder what would have happened if the woman had refused to come to Jesus when he called her. What if she felt too unworthy or afraid? What if she had not allowed him to touch her or didn't believe him when he called her "dear"? Sometimes we do cower when God calls us to him. We don't believe he's really calling our name. We're afraid of the changes healing would bring to our lives, or we feel so guilty or so unworthy that we decide we'd rather stay doubled over for 18 more years than hope that God will change us.

Recently while speaking for a women's group, a widow who knew God well shared her favorite verse with everyone: "Your Creator will be your husband; the LORD of Heaven's Armies is his name! He is your Redeemer, the Holy One of Israel, the God of all the earth" (Isaiah 54:5). Afterward, a married woman whispered in her ear, "I wish I had your husband."

The good news is, this woman can, and so can we. God invites us all (even you, men) to have a personal and intimate relationship with him, the Creator, the Lord of heaven and earth. He promises us that he loves us more than the best husband or wife or parent or friend could, more than we can imagine (Ephesians 3:18-19). He tells us nothing could ever stop him from loving us, and that he is absolutely *for* us, not against us (Romans 8:31-39).

He sees you right where you are, and he knows your pain, but do you believe him when he says he loves you? God doesn't want you to merely see him differently than you have in the past—he wants you to interact with him differently. He is not a distant, disinterested deity or a cosmic cop eager to catch you doing wrong so he can punish you. How you see God determines how you will relate to him, as well as how you see yourself. Retreat director Richard Rohr says,

> The people who know God well—the mystics, the hermits, those who risk everything to find God—always meet a lover, not a dictator. God is never found to be an abusive father or a tyrannical mother, but always a lover who is more than we dared hope for. How different than the "account manager" that most people seem to worship.[2]

Healing Flows from Your Relationship with God

God's healing comes as he speaks to us with his words of truth and we take them into our heart (Psalm 107:20). Jesus tells us that he sacrificed himself for us so that we can be made holy (and whole) by his truth (John 17:17-19). But the kind of biblical truth we need for inner healing and change is not informational truth, it is transformational truth. We don't need more knowledge; we need more Presence. The only way I know to experience this depth of truth is through the regular practice of abiding with Christ, and surrendering to him. Let me explain.

As I mentioned earlier, my inner healing began when I first heard God speaking directly to my heart after my mother rejected me for the umpteenth time. I was already married and a mother myself. I was working part-time as a counselor in a secular setting but had been a Christian for over ten years. I knew that God loved me. I even taught others that God loved them. I believed this truth as best I could, but I didn't trust it or experience it as deeply as I needed to in order to let go of my pain and my anger, which grew out of my mother's contempt. When God spoke to my heart that evening, I didn't simply acknowledge what he told me, this time I surrendered to his loving truth.

Surrender takes place when we choose (with our will) to believe God and to trust what he tells us, even when our emotions don't quite line up. Jesus modeled this when he yielded to God the Father by surrendering his will to God's perfect plan, even though his emotions were reluctant (Luke 22:42-44). Jesus told me I was *his* child, *his* precious daughter, and that it was time to let go of my anger, my expectations for a different mom. He asked me to forgive her. When I said yes, I began to experience the deeper inner healing and freedom I longed for.

My journey of learning to abide and surrender has taken me a long time. I didn't always feel safe in God's presence, because I

QUIETING OURSELVES, ABIDING IN HIM

The Lord tells us the secret of abiding in him is to quiet ourselves, externally as well as internally, so that we can know he is with us and in us (Psalm 46:10). Isaiah knew this secret when he told the Israelites they would find God's strength in quietness and trust (Isaiah 30:15).

Getting to that quiet place internally as well as physically can be challenging. Richard Rohr notes that God is always with us, but our awareness of his presence is what's missing.[3] Sharpening our spiritual senses is one of the secrets to experiencing the peace that surpasses understanding, which God promises his children in the tumultuous tempest called life (Philippians 4:7).

The best way I know to practice God's presence and to quiet my body and mind is to sit still, then silently and slowly begin to mindfully breathe; I simply inhale through my nose and exhale through my mouth. After a little while of this rhythmic breathing, I begin to engage my imagination. I remember recently becoming aware that what I said to God felt as watery as skim milk. Going through the motions of prayer, I was mumbling sentences that I wasn't even conscious of. When I noticed my own fakeness, I invited Jesus to make himself more real to me. I imagined him sitting in my big red chair right behind me. I felt my tears well up and I began to talk to him, not with religious words but authentic words, pouring out my heart to him. For a long time I abided in and surrendered to his goodness, his love, and his best for my life. Breathing in his Presence, breathing out all my fears, worries, anxieties, anger, and everything else I needed to let go of.

didn't know him well and I wasn't sure I could trust him. We relate
to God much as we relate to others. Rohr comments, "Most don't
know how to surrender to God. How can we surrender unless we
believe there is someone trustworthy out there to surrender to?"[4]
God understands our problems with trust. That's why one phrase
that is repeated more than any other one throughout the Scriptures
is, "Don't be afraid." He wants us to believe and trust that he loves
us and has a master plan for our life.

Relational Healing Follows Spiritual Healing

Spiritual healing always translates into relational healing. We
are freed from living in fear and bondage to our brokenness, and
we grow into living according to God's perfect love more of the
time (1 John 4:16-18). Please don't be impatient with your own
progress. God knows just what you need.

Several years ago I got a new dog. My beloved Alexandra had
died, and as much as I didn't think I wanted the work of a new
pet, I felt lonely without one. But this time I didn't want a puppy.
I wanted a dog that was beyond the furniture-chewing and peeing-
on-the-rug stage. My husband and I contacted a breeder and found
she had just what were looking for, an eight-month-old dog that
was the color and gender we wanted. She was also house-trained.
Perfect, I thought.

When we went to see her, we weren't so sure. The dog was timid
and was not the least bit friendly. Instead of wagging her tail and
greeting us, she ran and hid. Gracie was a victim of a destructive
relationship with her previous owner, and she showed the effects.

My heart went out to her and I wanted to love her. We bought
her and took her home. In the car, she trembled the entire way.
When we stopped at McDonald's and bought her a hamburger, she
refused to eat it. Each day I would try to play with or pet Gracie,
but she remained aloof and distant. She startled at the slightest
noise. She peed on the rug a few times, and when I took her for

grooming, she bit the groomer twice. I feared she was too damaged to become a good pet.

But gradually, she began to believe that I was not going to hurt her, and she began to entrust her heart to me. It's been almost two years now, and Gracie is a wonderful dog. She doesn't bite people anymore, although she is a little aloof, especially with strange men. But she is devoted to me, and God has showed me a little picture of what it means to abide.

Gracie loves to be with me, anywhere, anyplace. She would rather be in my presence than eat or sleep. Nothing is more important to her than being with me; she follows me everywhere and I am never out of her sight. Gracie trusts me completely. I can put a piece of steak in her mouth, and if I want it back, she willingly surrenders it. She feels secure, safe, and loved, and that has allowed her to heal and to blossom into an awesome dog. When I travel or am out of the house, Gracie doesn't do as well. My presence is part of her well-being. My absence causes her distress.

Our God desires to rescue us from darkness, destruction, and despair. He wants to give us his light and love. He is ever present and says he will never leave us or forsake us. God does not need to be *more* present to us; we need to be *more aware* of his presence. Jesus says, "Remain in my love" (John 15:9). Don't leave it for a minute. The closer we stay to God, the healthier we will become.

Be forewarned. Satan knows the power of abiding and of surrender; therefore, he does whatever he can to keep us from experiencing God's Presence or trusting God with our lives. He distracts us with good things that keep us too busy to spend meaningful time with God. When that doesn't work, he tempts us to believe we need to hold on to our bitterness and anger in order to stay strong. He continually tries to deceive us into thinking that we can find happiness by indulging the pleasures of our flesh or pursuing something other than God. Satan also condemns us with accusations, half truths, and lies. He fills us with fear. His goal is to make us stay away from God instead of running to him. Satan knows remaining and resting in God's Presence empowers us to live differently.

The psalmist wrote, "My heart has heard you say, 'Come and talk with me.' And my heart responds, 'LORD, I am coming'" (Psalm 27:8). God invites you too. Come talk with him. Are you willing?

EXPERIENCING GOD'S HEALING PRESENCE

Following are a few passages to get you started with knowing God more intimately. Meditate on what they say to you. Be still and let God impress certain truths upon your heart. Write down what strikes you. When the Holy Spirit speaks to your heart, listen well, for he speaks healing words.

> In his unfailing love, my God will stand with me. He will let me look down in triumph on all my enemies (Psalm 59:10).

> O my people, trust in him at all times. Pour out your heart to him, for God is our refuge (Psalm 62:8).

> I cling to you; your strong right hand holds me securely (Psalm 63:8).

> Who will protect me from the wicked? Who will stand up for me against evildoers? Unless the LORD had helped me, I would soon have settled in the silence of the grave. I cried out, "I am slipping!" but your unfailing love, O LORD, supported me. When doubts filled my mind, your comfort gave me renewed hope and cheer (Psalm 94:16-19).

> "I have told you all this so that you may have peace in me. Here on earth you will have many trials and sorrows. But take heart, because I have overcome the world" (John 16:33).

I also encourage you to read larger portions of Scripture, and use your imagination to picture Jesus talking with you. It helps

to read the Bible aloud so that you can hear what God has to
say to you. A few of my favorites are Psalm 73, Psalm 91, Luke
15, Romans 8, and Ephesians 1. When the words of God do not
express your own feelings, consider what Rabbi Abraham Heschel
said when members of his synagogue complained that the words
of the liturgy did not express what they felt. He told them that
instead of expecting the liturgy to express what they feel, they
should learn to feel what the liturgy expressed.[5] When we meditate on and memorize God's truth, we invite its power to change
how we feel.

How We See Ourselves

Whenever Jesus spoke into the lives of others and they responded
to his grace and truth, their feelings changed, and then their hearts
began to change. Their eyes were opened and they not only saw
him differently, they began to see themselves differently.

Identity, or how we see ourselves, is forged in relationships. Even
before he understands any words, an infant gets a sense of himself
from his interactions with his mother and father. Do they respond
positively when he cries? Are they gentle with him when he can't
settle himself? Do they enjoy seeing him smile or try new things?
If so, he will begin to experience himself as lovable, valuable, and
capable. On the other hand, infants and children who do not experience a nurturing environment develop a picture of themselves that
increases their risk for future destructive relationships. Such interactions are familiar and comfortable.

The process of developing a sense of who we are, however, doesn't
end with childhood. As we saw from chapter 2, Brad viewed himself
as a competent, intelligent contributor to his workplace, but under
a new boss, he began to feel more and more insecure and unsure of
himself. At any time of life, when our closest relationships are with
destructive people, our very sense of self is damaged. When the
relationship is abusive, the effects can be devastating.

On the other hand, when we interact with individuals who encourage us and love us and we believe them to be genuine, our sense of self can begin to heal. God knows the destructiveness of sin in relationships. One of his purposes for the family of God (the church), is to promote interpersonal and individual healing as we learn to lavishly and warmly love one another as he has loved us (John 15:12).

Healing a Damaged Identity

Let's look at how Jesus healed the damaged identity of one simple woman as she allowed him to love her. This story appears in John 4. On a hot and dusty afternoon, Jesus spoke with a woman who was in a destructive relationship and had been in several before that. The woman was a Samaritan. This is important to know because Jews considered Samaritans garbage and never personally interacted with them. In addition to being a Samaritan, she was a woman. Men of that day often viewed women as property, not people, and consequently didn't treat women very well. No respectable Jew would talk with a woman alone, let alone a Samaritan woman. Perhaps even more astonishing was that this woman was living with a man who was not her husband. In fact, she had been with a number of different men over the years. Scripture doesn't say specifically, but it's probable that this woman was at the well alone that day because the other women of the village wouldn't associate with her. She was likely considered an immoral woman, yet Jesus stopped and had a rather lengthy conversation with her that changed her entire life.

Remember, we can know what God is like by watching Jesus. He must have been hot in that desert sun. His disciples left him to buy food, and we know he was tired and thirsty, but he wasn't too tired to give his attention to one lonely, hurting woman who I'm sure felt labeled as undeserving of anything good.

Jesus opened the conversation by asking her for a drink. He treated her like a person, not a servant or unworthy sinner. He engaged her in a stimulating dialogue—the same kind of dialogue he had with Nicodemus, a learned religious leader—and showed her that she was important to him in spite of her gender, background, or sins. Then he offered her something wonderful—living water—so that she would not thirst for the wrong kind of love anymore. When they finished talking, she was so completely captivated by Christ, she left her water jug and ran back to the town to tell people about Jesus.

Here is a woman who came to the well that dusty afternoon seeing herself as an unworthy outcast. When she returned to her town, she knew she was loved and had a purpose. Her view of herself changed in that single, simple encounter with the One who loved her well. And, as we read in the story, we know her neighbors saw the change too; many came to believe in Jesus because of what she had to say.

In the same way, when Jesus met Peter, Peter saw himself as a fisherman, but Jesus saw Peter as a fisher of men (Matthew 4:18-19 NIV). After Peter betrayed Christ, Peter saw himself as a failure, but Jesus always saw Peter as a rock (Matthew 16:18). After Christ's resurrection we see a maturing Peter in Acts 2. As he addresses the crowd and explains who Jesus is, he quotes David from the Old Testament: "I saw the Lord always before me. Because he is at my right hand, I will not be shaken. Therefore my heart is glad and my tongue rejoices; my body also will live in hope" (Acts 2:25-26 NIV).

What changed Peter from a shaking coward or an impulsive, uneducated man to a bold and courageous fisher of men within just a few months of Christ's ascension? Prior to Christ's resurrection, Peter knew Jesus as his friend, his teacher, and his rabbi, but everything became crystal clear for Peter after he experienced Christ as his Lord, all powerful, always present. When Peter saw Jesus differently, he also saw himself differently, and he grew into the man Jesus said he was.

The apostle John usually identified himself not by his name, but by saying he was simply the disciple that Jesus loved. Can you say the same thing? That you are a woman or man whom Jesus loves?

When Jesus was on earth, few people saw him for who he truly was: the wonderful Messiah, the Lord God. Most hoped he would be Israel's next king and save the Jews from the Roman oppression. Others saw him as a fraud, some even as a kook. But Jesus' identity was secured in his Father's words, "You are my dearly loved Son, and you bring me great joy" (Luke 3:22). His Father's words kept him from forgetting who he was in the midst of the pressure to overthrow kingdoms, or while enduring the criticism and contempt of his abusers.

Who Do You Say I Am, Lord?

The question that heals distortions of our identity isn't a question we should ask of others or even of ourselves. It is, *Who do you say that I am, Lord?* The answer, if you believe what he says, can change your life.

Here are a few examples of what God says about us. Read each one aloud and ask yourself whether you believe it. If not, be honest, but write out why not. Then talk with God about your struggle. He never lies, so if he says it, it's true. But if God sees you in a way you don't yet see yourself, be patient. God wants to help you, like Peter, heal and grow up spiritually and emotionally so that you will become what you already are in his eyes.

> Anyone who harms you harms my most precious possession (Zechariah 2:8).
>
> The LORD your God is living among you. He is a mighty savior. He will take delight in you with gladness. With his love, he will calm all your fears. He will rejoice over you with joyful songs (Zephaniah 3:17).
>
> The LORD is compassionate and merciful, slow to get angry and filled with unfailing love. He will not constantly

accuse us, nor remain angry forever. He does not punish us for all our sins; he does not deal harshly with us, as we deserve. For his unfailing love toward those who fear him is as great as the height of the heavens above the earth. He has removed our sins as far from us as the east is from the west. The LORD is like a father to his children, tender and compassionate to those who fear him. For he knows how weak we are; he remembers we are only dust (Psalm 103:8-14).

"I know the plans I have for you," says the LORD. "They are plans for good and not for disaster, to give you a future and a hope" (Jeremiah 29:11).

Even before he made the world, God loved us and chose us in Christ to be holy and without fault in his eyes. God decided in advance to adopt us into his own family by bringing us to himself through Jesus Christ. This is what he wanted to do, and it gave him great pleasure (Ephesians 1:4-5).

This includes you who were once far away from God. You were his enemies, separated from him by your evil thoughts and actions. Yet now he has reconciled you to himself through the death of Christ in his physical body. As a result, he has brought you into his own presence, and you are holy and blameless as you stand before him without a single fault (Colossians 1:21-22).

Now there is no condemnation for those who belong to Christ Jesus (Romans 8:1).

We are God's masterpiece. He has created us anew in Christ Jesus so we can do the good things he planned for us long ago (Ephesians 2:10).

Long ago the LORD said to Israel: "I have loved you, my people, with an everlasting love. With unfailing love I have drawn you to myself" (Jeremiah 31:3).

Healing doesn't simply involve feeling better about who we are or who God is. True healing happens as we learn to live holy lives by growing into the identities God has already given us, which is what will make us whole. In the next chapter, we'll take a look at a woman who learned how to do this while married to a destructive man. Her name was Abigail.

If You Let Go, You Will Grow

He that respects himself is safe from others;
he wears a coat of mail that none can pierce.

HENRY W. LONGFELLOW

If you make the LORD your refuge,
if you make the Most High your shelter,
no evil will conquer you.

PSALM 91:9-10

A bigail was married to a foolish and cruel man. Her husband, Nabal, was wealthy but selfish. While David was fleeing King Saul, he and his men camped for a time where Nabal's servants were herding sheep. Chapter 25 in 1 Samuel tells us that David's entourage treated Nabal's shepherds honorably, and David expected Nabal to be grateful and hospitable in return. Rather than being thankful for David's protection, however, Nabal insulted him by disrespecting David's greeting and refusing his request for provisions.

David did not respond well to Nabal's stingy and disrespectful behavior. Enraged, he swore vengeance on Nabal's entire household. One of the servants saw what happened and ran to tell Abigail. He begged her to come up with a plan, because he knew it was useless to talk to Nabal. He said, "He is such a wicked man that no one can talk to him" (1 Samuel 25:17 NIV).

Although Abigail was married to a destructive person, she is described as both beautiful and intelligent. Her servant affirms this when he trusts that she will figure out what to do next. Abigail wasted no time; she knew what she must do and quickly did it. First, she prepared a feast to take to David and his men. She sent her servants out ahead of her, but she did not inform her husband what she planned.

Meanwhile, David worked himself into a rage as he brooded over Nabal's sarcasm and mistreatment. As Abigail entered the ravine, she saw David, thirsty for vengeance, getting ready to massacre every male in Nabal's household. She scrambled off her mule and bowed herself low before him.

Abigail began to speak, but she did not make excuses for her husband's poor behavior. She told it like it was: "I know Nabal is a wicked and ill-tempered man; please don't pay any attention to him. He is a fool, just as his name suggests" (verse 25). Miraculously, Abigail also takes responsibility for what happened. "I accept all blame in this matter, my lord," she said (verse 24). She protected her husband and her household by putting herself on the line.

We know that Abigail acted wisely and resourcefully by the way she handled the situation, but we also know that she feared God. She knew what to say to help David remember that he was God's anointed king, and she encouraged him to rethink his plan for vengeance. Abigail humbled herself before David and asked for his forgiveness, which allowed him to rise above his anger and trust God for justice against Nabal.

How did Abigail do it? What helped her survive as a person while in a toxic marriage? I'm certain that, just like any other woman, she longed for a husband who would cherish her. She stayed married, yet she did not allow her husband's selfishness, harshness, or foolishness to destroy her. She demonstrated remarkable presence of mind, resilience, and inner beauty in spite of her circumstances.

She chose to become a God-centered woman, and that choice kept her husband's wickedness from rubbing off on her.

Growth Requires Letting Go

Over the years, I've worked with women and men who, like Abigail, have healed and grown in spite of the destructive people around them. I'd like to tell you about some of the steps they have taken to enable that process to occur.

When we attempt to accomplish greater emotional and spiritual work, we usually think about the all things we need to *add* to our lives. We want to read and study the Bible, do meaningful ministry, gain greater emotional stability, better our interpersonal skills, or seek additional wisdom. All these endeavors can be helpful in our maturing process. But I have found in my own life as well as in my counseling practice that deeper and more lasting change usually comes about when we regularly practice letting go rather than doing more.

Recently I was speaking with Richard, a client, who feared God's judgment when he died because he wasn't working harder to do more. As we talked I said, "Perhaps we've gotten the concept of final judgment wrong. What if, in the end, Jesus isn't going to tell us everything we've ever done wrong or failed to do? What if he's going to show us the person we could have become and the things we would have done if only we allowed him to heal and mature us?"

Richard grew up in an abusive home. He struggled with residual anger and bitterness and felt stuck, unable to move beyond it. I asked him to close his eyes and imagine: "What would Jesus say you could become if you would only let go of your bitterness? Your resentment and hatred of your parents? Your fears? The lies you've believed?"

The writer of Hebrews tells us that if we want to lead a life well lived, we must "strip off every weight that slows us down, especially the sin that so easily trips us up" (Hebrews 12:1). The apostle Paul tells us to "throw off your old sinful nature and your former way of life, which is corrupted by lust and deception" (Ephesians 4:22). For Richard, as with all of us, the sins that trip us up are usually the things we so firmly cling to.

As Richard thought about all of this, he began to grasp the enormous cost he was paying to hold on to these things. Embracing his garbage didn't protect him from further hurt, nor did it pay back his abusers for their wrongdoing, but it did hinder him from growing into the person God intended him to be, and it kept him from living freely in the present.

Jesus once asked a man who was crippled, "Would you like to get well?" (John 5:6). The man replied that he couldn't do what was needed to be healed, and he gave a variety of reasons that seemed logical. Perhaps deep down he preferred his current suffering to the discipline that wholeness and maturity required.

Letting go in order to grow can be scary. It requires change, which demands a certain degree of faith and hope. That's why our picture of God must heal, at least a little, before we can embark on greater growth.

The writer of Hebrews reminds us that we can only let go and run the race of life well when we keep our eyes on Jesus. Abiding and surrender, the concepts I introduced in the previous chapter, continue to be important as we practice the discipline of letting go.

There are three things we must learn to let go of if we want greater healing and maturity in our lives.

Let Go of Unrealistic Expectations

One of the things that kept Abigail sane in her marriage was her deep roots in reality. She did not entertain any idealistic notions about her husband suddenly doing something noble or loving. She knew who he was, and that's who she expected him to be. Abigail was not shocked by Nabal's behavior toward David and his men.

Many individuals remain unhealthy in destructive relationships because they keep hoping that the other person will eventually become someone different. When that doesn't happen, they feel angry, hurt, disappointed, and frustrated because somehow they still expect change. One common definition of insanity is doing the same thing over and over again while expecting different results. First recognizing and then releasing our unrealistic expectations of others is a crucial element in gaining greater mental and emotional health.

I reached a turning point in my own life when I finally said goodbye to the hope that somehow my mother would change. I resisted doing this because I so desired her to be in my life, and I wanted her to apologize for all the pain she caused. I didn't want to accept that she might never see her problem, or that I couldn't make her see it, nor could I make her do anything about it even if she did see it.

Letting go of what we want feels horrible at first, much like grieving a death. I had to accept that my mother was not going to play the role I wanted her to play in my life. As we go through the normal stages of grieving from denial to anger and bargaining and finally to acceptance, we feel deep pain and sorrow. But in the end, going through the process empowers us to move on with our lives. Staying stuck in denial or anger doesn't help us live maturely or abundantly now.

You may be wondering why it was unrealistic of me to expect that my mother would want to be involved in my life. Most mothers do want to be close with their children. Likewise, many married people expect that their spouses will treat them honorably and lovingly, and there is nothing wrong with that. Our expectations only become problematic when they don't align with what's real or true. A healthy person always accepts reality and truth over fantasy and wishful thinking, even if it's quite painful.

Recently I saw three white crosses planted alongside a roadway, a poignant reminder of the three teenagers who lost their lives in a tragic automobile accident. Along with the crosses were flowers, stuffed animals, photos, and cards, mementos left by friends and loved ones struggling to accept the harsh reality of these untimely deaths. These symbols were helpful to everyone who needed to face the truth and say goodbye. If however, we came upon this scene six months later and saw people still sitting on the grass, holding on to the stuffed animals, we would surely think something is dreadfully wrong.

Please don't misunderstand. I'm not saying that six months is enough time to erase grief. The point is, if we don't make some effort to embrace reality and let go of disappointment, even when it's hard, we can't move on. The process takes time and is difficult, but spring always comes after winter, and new life buds when we let our unrealistic expectations die.

Entitlement

For some of us, letting go is unusually difficult because we feel entitled to have the things we want. Our culture certainly reinforces the idea that we deserve these things. *Why shouldn't I have the kind of mother I long for? Why doesn't God give me a better spouse? I'm not asking for anything unreasonable.* This line of thought, though understandable, is emotionally destructive to us. It breeds discontent, resentment, and self-pity, which are lethal to our maturity and well-being. It also causes us to question God's goodness and sovereignty, which hinders our spiritual lives.

When, as we learned in chapter 7, we take responsibility for our problems, we often see that our problem is that our

PAYING ATTENTION TO THE GOOD THINGS

One exercise that I practice to change the unrealistic ways I look at my circumstances is to take a moment to review each day, identify three good things that happened, and look for the reason why.[1] Studies have shown that individuals who tend to notice the good in their lives live happier as well as longer. As humans we are not omniscient. We cannot pay attention to everything, and so by nature, we pay selective attention to life. Some say we create much of our own reality. Those who unconsciously attend more to the negative things feel more unhappy and discontent. When we consciously learn to pay attention to the good and positive things in life, we feel better.

expectations don't match up with reality, and we don't like it. What are you going to do about the expectations that are holding you back? Are you going to take steps to change what you can (always a good start)? What will you do with the things you cannot change? Either you will continue to be upset, and grumble and complain, or you can choose to surrender those things to God and learn to be content. The apostle Paul learned these lessons while sitting in prison (Philippians 4:11-12). Abigail released her expectations for a loving husband without bitterness, and she was mentally, emotionally, and spiritually stronger because of her choice.

Many psychological studies today confirm what the apostle Paul taught us almost two thousand years earlier. He said, "Fix your thoughts on what is true, and honorable, and right, and pure, and lovely, and admirable. Think about things that are excellent and worthy of praise" (Philippians 4:8). He also reminded us to "be thankful in all circumstances, for this is God's will for you who belong to Christ Jesus" (1 Thessalonians 5:18).

Let Go of Negative Emotions

As we practice letting go of our unrealistic expectations, we may still fight negative feelings that we can't shake. Richard did not have any expectations about a better relationship with his parents, but he stayed stuck because he allowed his understandable anger and hurt to harden into bitterness, hatred, and strong resentment. These negative emotions colored his mood and shaped his disposition, which in turn disrupted his present life. In order for Richard to grow healthier, he needed to learn how to release his destructive feelings.

It's amazing how ensnared we become by our negative emotions and moods, and how helpless we feel to move beyond them. But each of us knows how to let them go when we need to. One day I felt rather cranky and miserable and let everyone around me know it. Then the phone rang. When I answered it, I heard myself say in the sweetest tone, "Hello." Suddenly I got it. For a phone call, I let go of my negative feelings. After the phone conversation, I noticed my crankiness was not nearly as potent. Now don't get me wrong: I could have easily revved it back up, but that time I chose to let it go entirely. As a result, I had a much better day, as did the people around me.

Some people choose to hold on to their resentment, believing that staying mad is a way of punishing the offender. That's what Richard was doing. He didn't want to forgive his parents or let go of his bitterness. He wanted them to pay for what they did to him. Of course, his parents weren't paying the price; he was, as were his wife and children.

Having emotional and spiritual maturity doesn't mean we don't feel our emotions when someone treats us poorly. Becoming whole and holy means we don't retaliate or seek revenge when they do. We forgive them and do them good, not harm, even if the relationship is broken.

Jesus shows us what full maturity (wholeness and holiness) looks like. He felt hurt and sad when he was mistreated and abused, but he didn't revile in return (1 Peter 2:22). He felt brokenhearted when those he loved treated him with indifference, but he did not turn away or reject them (Matthew 23:37). Jesus did not have relationship with these individuals, but he never turned his back on them either. He always faced forward, acted in their best interests, and continued to invite them into repentance *and* into relationship. He is our example to strive toward.

Perhaps some of the most toxic and destructive emotions that we have difficulty letting go of are our own shame and self-hatred. People in destructive relationships experience a great deal of shame. Shame for failing to keep their relationships intact, shame for being rejected *(I wasn't good enough, pretty enough, young enough, smart enough, thin enough, spiritual enough),* shame for being unloved, and shame for not stopping what they allowed to happen. If you are a victim of your own shame and self-hatred, you are your own worst enemy. The one person most hindering you from becoming all God says you can be is you. Please learn to release these negative emotions so that you can heal. Otherwise they will slowly poison your spirit, soul, and body.

How to Do It

Now that you know you need to let go of these negative emotions, how do you actually do it? The very first step is to make the choice to do so. Bringing your will in line is the most important part of this process. Without it, your emotions will never cooperate. Decide, *I will no longer allow these destructive emotions to run roughshod over my life. I will work, and when necessary, work hard, to release them.*

David wrote the psalms to help him process and let go of his emotions. As we read them, we often discover that the first part of the psalm is a complaint, a fear, a hurt, or a question. As David works through his honest feelings, we see that by the end of the psalm he is often feeling better. Keep a daily journal and honestly face what you feel. Don't be afraid of your feelings, but ask them a question: *Why are you here?* Allow yourself to be with your feelings for a time, and invite Jesus to speak to your heart. Perhaps he will comfort you, or remind you of his love for you, or even give you a piece of his Word as healing truth. As you show compassion and care for your sadness or anger, release it to God and ask him to heal you.

Forgiveness is also a powerful release for toxic emotions. When you forgive, the anger or resentment you're entitled to no longer captivates you. When you forgive, you set the prisoner free and the prisoner is *you.* You give the offender over to God to handle as he deems just. Although Abigail was realistic about her husband, we don't detect a hint of bitterness in her tone. He was who he was, but Abigail was free to do him good because she had already let go of any bitterness and resentment; she forgave his shortcomings and sins. Forgiving someone might lead to reconciliation of a relationship, especially if the person you forgive repents and changes, but it doesn't always.[2]

Sometimes we let go and forgive, then find our bad feelings resurfacing a while later. Or we don't know why we feel what we do, but we're miserable. Now what? Remember, you have an enemy (Satan), who wants to rob you of anything good. We must fight him, and here is one way you can. (Additional ways of fighting Satan will be covered in the next chapter.) When your negative feelings get the better of you, intentionally switch your emotional channel. Practice something completely opposite of the way you feel. Reengage your will in the decision to let go.

One day I was feeling exhausted and discouraged. Instead of giving in to those feelings, I put on some peppy music and started washing the dishes. Before long I found myself singing to the music and dancing around the kitchen with my dog. Studies show that when we choose to do something positive, even smile, our brain signals a shift in our emotions, and we often feel better.[3] Try it. The Bible reminds us that "a cheerful heart is good medicine" (Proverbs 17:22).

Doing something kind or helpful for someone else can also lift our spirits. After her divorce, Barbara's adult children chose to spend the holidays with their father. Instead of staying home, feeling sorry for herself and eating a frozen dinner alone (which she was tempted to do), Barbara volunteered to serve the poor a holiday meal. As we serve others, we often find that we receive joy, which makes us feel better.[4] Service takes our eyes off our own problems and feelings for a time and helps us appreciate the good aspects of our lives.

If destructive feelings become a regular part of your life, especially depression, suicidal thoughts, self-hatred or rage, please consider professional counseling. Don't hinder your growth because you're too proud or too ashamed to ask for help. The right therapist can make all the difference in your journey toward greater growth.

Let Go of Lies

We learned in chapter 3 that because of our brokenness, we are especially susceptible to lies (Romans 1:25). Psychiatrist Scott Peck says, "One of the roots of mental illness is invariably an interlocking system of lies that we have been told and lies that we tell ourselves."[5]

As I've explained, when someone has been in a destructive relationship for any length of time, especially as a child, lies may *feel* more real than the truth does. But it's crucial for your mental, spiritual, and emotional heath that you learn to detect the lies you have been told, the lies you tell yourself, and the lies you believe, and then replace them with the truth. If you have been told repeatedly that you're stupid, ugly, incapable, or worthless by those you thought cared about you, it's extremely difficult not to believe it, at least a little bit. When you believe the lie that you are small and others are big, you feel helpless and powerless.

One of my favorite childhood movies was *The Wizard of Oz*. When Dorothy approached the wizard, he frightened her. He made everyone believe he was big and powerful. But one day when the wizard was ranting and raving about how powerful he was, Dorothy's little dog, Toto, wandered behind the curtain and exposed the truth. This supposedly powerful man wasn't a wizard at all, nor was he very big. The truth was that he was a rather small, ordinary man, who only pretended he was big.

Like the wizard, many verbally abusive people appear larger than life to us. Their intent is to make us believe that they are so strong and powerful, we'd better do exactly what they say. The truth is that they are mere mortals, and their ranting and raging is a cover for their own smallness. They only appear large if we believe we are small and helpless. If you want to break free from their grasp, you must let go of that lie.

Deceit can be blatant or subtle. Satan is the Father of Lies, and deceitful words are his weapon of choice. He masterfully twists reality so that wrong appears right, good looks bad, and evil seems virtuous. But sometimes even Christians are guilty of twisting truth into lies to serve their own purposes. The only way we can discern truth is to listen to God and read his Word in context. The psalmist cried out,

> Show me the right path, O LORD; point out the road for me to follow. Lead me by your truth and teach me, for you are the God who saves me. All day long I put my hope in you (Psalm 25:4-5).

To mature, all believers must submit themselves to the renewal of their minds. Even if we haven't been subjected to destructive relationships, God says we all need to put off our old ways of thinking and believing. It's just as detrimental to our spiritual and emotional maturity to think we're entitled, deserving, and more special than others as it is to think we're inferior and worthless. We all need to root out the lies that shape us: lies about ourselves, lies about God, lies about others, and lies about life.

James warns us that when we are doubled-minded, we become unstable (James 1:6-7). This describes the person who knows something at one level and doubts it on another. We have faith intellectually that God loves us, but our hearts don't quite believe it. Why not? Because we are subject to an internal lie that we have not faced or renounced. It's crucial to our healing as well as to our maturity that we uproot these lies rather than simply teaching our minds new truths.

Recognize and Identify Lies

How do we let go of lies? First, we must recognize and identify them. Peter instructed fellow believers to "rid yourself of all malice and all *deceit,* hypocrisy, envy, and slander of every kind. Like newborn babies, crave pure spiritual milk, so that by it you may grow up in your *salvation*" (1 Peter 2:1-2 NIV). Peter teaches we must let go of the old in order to take in the new. The apostle Paul encourages believers to "continue to work out your *salvation* with fear and trembling" (Philippians 2:12 NIV). Both Peter and Paul say that our salvation is both a once-and-done event, as well as an ongoing process in which we play an important part.

The Greek word for salvation *(soteria)* means "deliverance," "preservation," and "safety," but it is not limited to the spiritual dimension of life. Salvation includes the restoration or healing of the whole person, mind, body, and spirit. An additional way that *soteria* can be translated is as "a deliverance from the molestation of enemies." [6] Let's look at what Peter and Paul said again, translating *salvation* this way.

> Rid yourself of all malice and all deceit, hypocrisy, envy, and slander of every kind. Like newborn babies, crave pure spiritual milk, so that by it you may grow up in your *[deliverance from the molestation of enemies]*" (1 Peter 2:1-2 NIV).
>
> Continue to work out your *[deliverance from the molestation of enemies]* with fear and trembling (Philippians 2:12 NIV).

What a promise! Healing is possible for those of us who were bruised and damaged by the molestation of destructive people. The apostle Paul continues to instruct us in this process of maturing. He says, "Let the word of Christ dwell in you richly" (Colossians 3:16 NIV). We only clearly recognize the lies we are tangled in as we grow more and more familiar with the truth. Become a student of God's Word, not academically but personally. As you read a passage, ask yourself if you believe it. If not, why not? As we have already learned, we can talk honestly to God about our doubts. Confess your unbelief and ask him to increase your trust so that you can more fully believe what he tells you.

Practice Living in the Truth

Another way to grow in truth and let go of lies is to practice living or walking in the truth, even if you don't believe it quite yet.

Throughout the Scriptures we are exhorted to walk in the truth, and that begins with a step of faith. As I write this, I'm preparing for a teaching trip to Iraq. I'm walking in the truth that the Lord will go with me and before me. I am surrounded by his love whether I am in Pennsylvania or in Iraq. But am I a little scared? You bet! Courage isn't the absence of fear but the faith to walk through the fear. As I take small steps of faith, trusting in God and what he tells me, my faith grows steadier and stronger.

We began to learn this discipline in chapter 10, but we must continue to practice it. If you're not quite convinced that you are fearfully and wonderfully made, walk in that truth and act as if you already believe it (Psalm 139:13-17). How would you see yourself differently if you *did* believe it? Most likely you'd feel more confident, more worthwhile, more purposeful, more beautiful (or handsome), and more loved.

What would be different about you if you walked through your day as if you believed that you could do all things through Christ as he gives you strength (Philippians 4:13)? How might that truth help you to take responsibility for making changes in your life? What would you say as you speak the truth in love to someone? What boundaries or limits would you have the courage to set? Or what new ministry or service would you do?

We cannot live like the daughters or sons of a king and act like an orphan at the same time. We will live in one world or another, depending on whose version of truth we're listening to and believing. Work diligently to let go of lies and believe God.

Gaining by Losing

The spiritual life is often a strange paradox. The way up is down; the first shall be last; to be full we must empty ourselves; to live we must first die; to find ourselves we must lose ourselves; and we gain more not by adding more, but by letting go.

Real life, as well as nature, is often a metaphor of deeper spiritual truths. On a popular program on television, called *The Biggest*

Loser, overweight contestants from around the country compete to see who can lose the most weight. This season I watched several episodes. The transformation of the participants was amazing, not only physically, but mentally and emotionally as well.

Week by week, as they let go of their favorite foods, they gained a healthier body. Some significantly lowered their blood sugar and blood pressure levels, as well as their cholesterol counts. They let go of their right to eat as much as they wanted, and as a result, they gained a slimmer physique, some losing more than a hundred pounds. When they gave up their leisure time to exercise, they gained strong muscle. They let go of the lie that they couldn't do it and gained self-discipline, self-confidence, and self-respect. They lost the weight and gained a healthier, happier life.

In one episode, the contestants were challenged to run a race. But the task wasn't as simple as it seemed. Each person had to wear a special belt. Clipped to that belt were weights in all the increments that they had lost each week. Some contestants had to run with sixty additional pounds clipped to their belts. At the end of the race, the weights were removed. It was a poignant reminder of how difficult their lives had been when they carried all that extra body weight. In the race, the excess hindered them from running at their best pace. The larger meaning was equally obvious: Their former weight had kept them from living their lives well.

You may find you need to let go of many things. Hanging on to unrealistic expectations, to damaging emotions, and to lies is like trying to run the race of life with weights attached to your belt. They slow you down, tire you out, and may even convince you that you can't make it.

Make a promise to yourself to regain your life by letting go. Then practice letting go of the things you know are weighing you down. Don't worry about everything you don't know about yet. God is patient with us. He knows growth and maturity take time. I'm still learning to let go. It is a lifelong process, but be encouraged. The lighter you get, the freer you are.

One of my friends wrote this poem and granted me permission to print it here:

From the ashes of heartache
A soul will arise
On the wings of a warrior
With merciful eyes.

With the ointment of truth
The gift of His grace
His love gently rains
On my wounds and remains.

He's the shield of my heart
Inner strength He imparts
To help me live a life
That brings glory to Christ.

—DONNA UPSON, 2006

When You're Properly Nourished, You Will Thrive

Wisdom sees everything in focus.

A.W. TOZER

The thief's purpose is to steal and kill and destroy.
My purpose is to give them a rich and satisfying life.

JOHN 10:10

I f you ever stop growing, you're physically, emotionally, mentally, or spiritually dying or dead. Several years ago I talked with a nursery specialist who told me a story about a tree that stopped growing. She dug around the trunk to inspect the roots, and she found that the tree wasn't able to receive the proper nourishment because its roots were entirely wrapped around the ball of the tree. Instead of growing outward, they grew inward.

Her story reminded me of some of the individuals I've worked with. They become tangled in their own inner thoughts and feelings, needs and desires, past injuries and hurts. When that happens, like the root-bound tree, they can't seek or receive the nourishment available to them from God or others so that they might grow.

What had to be done in order for the tree to begin to grow

again? The tree's roots had to be cut in order to free them. Initially the tree went into shock and actually got a little worse. But over time, and with some additional fertilizer and care, it began to thrive.

As we let go of the things we need to let die, we also need to surround ourselves with the proper nutrients so that we can thrive.

Build a Good Support System

One of the unrealistic expectations that I hope you have let go of by now is that there is one person out there somewhere who can meet all of your needs or wants and be there for you all of the time. That is a fantasy left over from infancy. Let it die. Even a wonderful mother eventually fails to meet her children's every need. Sooner or later she says no to a request or is not available when needed. That doesn't mean she doesn't love her children or that they aren't important to her. It means that her children are not the center of her world. It also might indicate that she was teaching them how to stand on their own two feet, which is a good thing to learn.

Letting go of that fantasy doesn't mean people aren't important or that we don't need them in our lives. We do. We need individuals who will support us, encourage us, be honest with us, help us, hold us accountable to our goals, pray with us, teach us, comfort us, celebrate with us, and help us see more clearly. But there is no one person who will do all of these functions for us every time we want them to. That's why it's important to build a network of different people that we can draw from. Some might be in professional roles such as pastors, counselors, or teachers. Others might be friends, co-workers, neighbors, spouses, or relatives.

When your support person says, "No, I can't be there for you right now," that doesn't mean he or she doesn't care for you. But it *does* mean you may need to call on someone else for help in that moment, or that you need to learn to handle your need by yourself (with God's help). When you lean too heavily one on person, or on people in general, your dependency will become destructive to you and your relationships.

In chapter 6, I encouraged you to start thinking of people who could support you as you learned to stop the destructiveness. Now think of people who will support your growth. Your list may include the same people, or you may want to add new names. If you need a mentor, a coach, accountability partners, or a Christian counselor, don't be afraid to ask someone directly. Most of the time, people appreciate being asked, even if they can't accommodate you immediately. Also, many of these same people can refer you to someone who is available to help.

Educate Yourself

As you recover and heal from the aftermath of a destructive relationship or person, you may struggle with labels you have been given during that experience. One woman came to counseling because her husband had convinced her she was sexually defective. She couldn't climax with him, and he told her it was because of her previous sexual abuse. She was damaged goods. When I asked her questions and got specific details, however, I realized that her sexual dysfunction was nothing out of the ordinary. Many women experience exactly what she did with no history of sexual abuse. Her husband was misinformed, and so was she. The relief that spread over her face when I pulled out a simple book on female sexuality and anatomy and showed her the facts was priceless.

Another one of my clients is fighting for her sanity as her husband deceives the people around her into believing that she is mentally ill. Court-ordered counselors as well as custody evaluators and judges don't always recognize the symptoms of traumatized women. An emotionally battered woman's hysterical efforts to be heard are often misdiagnosed as bipolar illness, borderline personality disorder, or worse.

If someone tells you that you have a problem, don't automatically write them off. On the other hand, don't automatically believe what they say. Educate yourself. Research the Internet, go to the library, read about the actual symptoms of the particular problem. Don't stay in denial if you indeed do have this problem. Get the help you need. On the other hand, there may be another explanation. What a relief to learn that your symptoms may have another name.

Many churches offer support groups as well as classes on addictions, the aftermath of divorce, depression, marriage enrichment, parenting, and caregiving for elderly parents, as well as Bible studies. Avail yourself of these opportunities to connect with others, and to learn and practice the things that will help you grow into a healthier, more mature person.

Learn to Handle Conflict

Conflict is a normal part of life, because people are different from one another and don't always see issues the same way or have the same goals. Conflict is always about an issue. If someone is picking on you or putting you down, you are not experiencing conflict; you are experiencing disrespect or abuse. When this happens, do not engage in a debate or defend yourself. Simply speak up and say, "Stop. I don't like it when you pick on me or put me down." If the other person refuses to stop, follow the steps you learned in chapters 8 and 9: Stand up and step back.

When there is a variance of opinion, or when two people want different things, then healthy conflict may result. In Acts 15, we read of a hot debate about whether the Gentiles should be circumcised and afforded the same status as Jewish believers. Around the same time, the apostle Paul and Barnabas disagreed over whether to take John Mark on one of their missionary journeys. Paul felt they shouldn't; Barnabas thought they should. They agreed to disagree and parted ways.

BIBLICAL RESOLUTION OF CONFLICTS

Here are some basic rules you can follow in order to resolve conflict biblically.

- *Define the problem or conflict to be discussed and stick to the issue.* Many disagreements get nowhere or deteriorate into brawls because the issue that started the conflict becomes lost in the midst of ugly words, past problems, or hurts that are thrown into the discussion.

- *When possible, plan a time for the discussion.* Preparing for fights isn't always possible, because sometimes they just erupt. But if you know you need to address a touchy issue, make a time to discuss it when both parties are rested and ready. It's difficult to fight fairly and constructively when you're tired, stressed out, and distracted with other obligations.

- *Listen carefully to the other person's perspective.* Show attentiveness and respect with both your body language and words (James 1:19; Proverbs 18:2).

- *Aim for a solution that works for both of you.* Your relationship is more important than the issue. Fighting to get your way or to prove you're right is not godly (Philippians 2:2-3; James 4:1-3). On the other hand, giving in because you're intimidated or afraid isn't good for the relationship either.

- *Commit to do no harm* (1 Corinthians 13:4-8; Romans 13:10). We are to love our neighbor as ourselves. Our spouses, by the way, are our closest neighbors.

- *Tame your tongue.* As we've learned, words can heal and can wound (Proverbs 12:18). Do not use your tongue as a weapon to attack someone (Matthew 5:22). Pay attention to your tone and body language. Do they communicate caring and openness or defensiveness and hostility (Proverbs 25:20; 29:11; 1 Peter 2:17)?

- *If you are unable to fight fairly, or the other person is attacking, stop.* Take a time-out until you can be constructive, but make a plan to return to the issue. Don't ignore it, hoping it will go away. If the other person will not stop attacking, seek a mediator or third person who can be objective.

- *If the other person breaks these rules, don't react in kind* (Proverbs 15:1). Relationships deteriorate pretty rapidly when two sinners sin against each other at the same time (Galatians 5:13-15). Refuse to engage if the other person will not stick to the rules of fair fighting.[1]

See Your Goodness and Find Your Strengths

As we saw in chapter 3, many people are blind to their brokenness. On the other hand, those in a relationship with a destructive person often see nothing but their own brokenness and are blind to their positive qualities. Although all humankind is broken, we are also blessed with incredible goodness, beauty, and strength. We are created in God's image, and he has put good things inside of us. It is not prideful to acknowledge them and appreciate them, especially if we use them to serve God and others.

In order to thrive, we don't just need to get rid of the bad stuff, we need to recognize and nurture the good qualities inside of us. Make a list of the strengths you have, not in spite of what you've endured, but because of it. Perhaps you have become resourceful or tenacious. Maybe you've learned how to look at the humor in situations and can laugh at yourself. You might have persistence or great endurance or patience.

I gave this assignment to one of my clients as she was healing from a destructive marriage. When she did it, she was surprised to discover how many strengths she had. I liken this exercise to hidden-pictures challenges often found in children's magazines.

You look at a picture, whether a photo or a drawing, and at first glance, you see it one way. The picture is accompanied by a list of items embedded within the picture. If you look carefully enough, you will find them. Discovering your strengths in the midst of the ruins of a relationship isn't always easy. You might have to search for them at first, but once you see them, they're obvious.

In addition to the strengths you've developed, begin to notice or recall the gifts and abilities you once had. You might have been musically inclined or good at math. Or perhaps you're socially comfortable and can talk with anyone, anywhere, but you've lost your confidence because of the destructive relationship you've been in. Brad (chapter 2) doubted some of his natural business talents and abilities under the critical and demeaning eye of his new boss. Once he freed himself from that destructive relationship, it didn't take long for him to remember them and reclaim them for himself.

Once you call to mind your gifts and abilities, take the time to nurture them. Most of our gifts don't present themselves in their mature state. A gifted musician still needs music lessons and hours of practice. A talented athlete needs coaching and lots of playing time in order to develop even natural abilities. The apostle Paul encouraged young Timothy not to neglect his gifts, but to be diligent and to "fan into flames" the gift God gave him (1 Timothy 4:14-15; 2 Timothy 1:6).

At this juncture in your healing, you must take time to nourish your growth and put yourself in the company of others who will encourage your maturity. You can do this even if you are not totally free from your destructive relationship. Remember, Abigail thrived even though she was married to a destructive man.

Let's look at how to be in the presence of destructive people without letting them or their behavior get the best of us.

Interacting with a Destructive Person

Like Abigail did, it is crucial that you learn how to interact with a destructive person without getting destroyed. Even if you are no longer in close relationship with this person, you might still have encounters. Divorced parents, for example, may need to interact on behalf of their children. When the other person is a family member, whether by blood or the family of God, at times you will be in the same place together. Start to prepare and practice for these meetings. The apostle Paul warned young Timothy about how to handle a destructive person. He said, "Alexander the metalworker did me a great deal of harm. The Lord will repay him for what he has done. You too should be on your guard against him, because he strongly opposed our message" (2 Timothy 4:14-15 NIV).

We learn from this passage that Alexander did not merely oppose Paul's message, he personally harmed Paul. So Paul warned Timothy to be careful around the man. If we were to handle hazardous materials such as insecticide or dangerous chemicals, a wise person would put on appropriate clothing, like gloves and a mask, for protection. In the same way, when we are around toxic people, we must protect ourselves so that their toxicity does not infect us.

Preparation

If you know ahead of time that you will be encountering a person who has previously been abusive, controlling, deceitful, or indifferent toward you, you must mentally, emotionally, and spiritually prepare yourself. You wouldn't knowingly enter a hazardous environment without some forethought, so don't blindly walk into an obviously difficult situation without first making a plan.

When I went with my sister to Florida to see our hospitalized mother, I had been anticipating such a moment for a long time. I had forgiven her years earlier and, like Paul did with Alexander, I turned our relationship over to God. But now I needed to prepare myself to see her. What kinds of things might she say that would push my buttons? What did I need to do to mute my buttons so if she pushed, I wouldn't react?

Giving advance thought about how to best interact with a destructive person pays off in large dividends. One of my clients, Sally, knew that conversations with her ex-husband around any issue always left her feeling exhausted and angry. In spite of a great deal of growth, she still had trouble with allowing him to intimidate her into doing what she didn't want to do. As she prepared for a difficult discussion with him around some child-support issues, she decided to put her remarks in writing and send them via e-mail. She told him that because she found it difficult to have a constructive conversation with him, she wanted to have all future correspondence and conversation done through e-mail.

Sally took responsibility for her problem. She wasn't yet able to set boundaries that protected her in face-to-face meetings. She continued to allow her ex-husband to control her, so she came up with a plan to put limits on his contact with her. She created some distance so that she could respond more thoughtfully and appropriately. The added benefit was that her ex-husband now put his manipulative behavior and intimidating manner in writing, and Sally had a much easier time recognizing it and not falling prey to it.

If you must interact with someone you know is unsafe, whenever possible insist that a mediator or third party be present for all communication.

Practice

As I packed to go to Florida, I began to mentally role play all kinds of possible scenarios that might involve my mother. I knew her ways, and I also knew my own weaknesses. I rehearsed how I wanted to respond differently than I had in the past. If she provoked me, I wanted to be gracious and quiet, not taking her bait. If she was cold, I wanted to be patient and warm. If she began verbally assaulting me, I wanted to respond by inviting her to stop, and if she didn't, to not react in kind. As a person, I was growing to be more proactive instead of reactive in many areas of my life. If she treated me abusively, I did not want to repay her evil with more evil of my own. In this moment with my mother, God was testing my character growth, but I needed some practice and used my imagination to do so *prior* to actually seeing her.

In the past, if you have been reactive when someone pushes your buttons, step back both physically and emotionally in order to distance yourself. Treat the provocative person much like you would treat a stranger. Have no expectations of a positive encounter. Be cordial, respectful, and kind, but don't get too close. You'd be especially wary if you suspected that the stranger may be carrying a weapon. For destructive people, their tongues are their weapons.

If you have had difficulty implementing some of the steps outlined in chapters 8 and 9, enlist the help of a trusted friend or counselor in order to role play speaking up, standing up, and stepping back. Doing so will help you get used to saying the things you want to say and, as with everything else, the more you practice something, the more natural it becomes.

Prayer

The most important part of our preparation and protection against a destructive person isn't mental, it's spiritual. As we've already seen in chapter 6, behind every destructive individual stands a much bigger enemy. Satan wants to destroy us, and he'll use anyone who is available. Destructive individuals may not even be aware that they are his pawn, but we must be aware and on guard. The apostle Paul advises believers how to stand against evil:

> Be strong in the Lord and in his mighty power. Put on all of God's armor so that you will be able to stand firm against all strategies of the devil. For we are not fighting against flesh-and-blood enemies, but against evil rulers and authorities of the unseen world, against mighty powers in this dark world, and against evil spirits in the heavenly places.

Therefore, put on every piece of God's armor so you will be able to resist the enemy in the time of evil. Then after the battle you will still be standing firm. Stand your ground, putting on the belt of truth and the body armor of God's righteousness. For shoes, put on the peace that comes from the Good News so that you will be fully prepared. In addition to all of these, hold up the shield of faith to stop the fiery arrows of the devil. Put on salvation as your helmet, and take the sword of the Spirit, which is the word of God.

Pray in the Spirit at all times and on every occasion. Stay alert and be persistent in your prayers for all believers everywhere (Ephesians 6:10-18).

Spiritual armor protects us against evil, much like a hazmat suit protects its wearer from toxins in the environment. It's a good practice to remember to put it on every day, but intentionally put it on, piece by piece, when you know you will be in contact with a destructive person.

Remember, one of the surest signs of your own emotional and spiritual growth and maturity is that you no longer retaliate when someone hurts you or does wrong to you. One of the most natural things we feel when someone hurts us is to want vengeance or respond to evil with more evil of our own. But Jesus specifically commands us to respond radically differently than our natural selves would. He calls us to love our enemies and do them good, not harm (Matthew 5:43-45).

Overcoming Evil with Good

Throughout his epistles, the apostle Paul gives us specific instructions on dealing with all kinds of people and relationship problems, but he sums up much of his teaching with this powerful advice, "Do not be overcome by evil, but overcome evil with good" (Romans 12:21 NIV). Let's look more specifically at this command

and how we can implement it while relating with a destructive person.

Overcome is a fighting word. It means to "prevail" or "conquer." I believe that's what Abigail learned to do. Her humble hospitality in response to David's threat of vengeance influenced him to change his mind. On the other hand, we have no evidence that her goodness ever changed her husband's ways. (Neither do we know what he would have been like without Abigail's presence in his life.) But the person most changed by Abigail's decision to overcome evil with good was Abigail. She was not embittered by her husband's destructiveness, nor was she intimidated or paralyzed with fear by her husband's foolishness or David's thirst for vengeance. She handled herself with a wise combination of grace and truth.

There are times when doing good will influence others to stop or pause to think about their destructive behaviors. Other times, doing good won't seem to make any difference at all, and in fact, circumstances may actually get worse. However, like an effective antidote neutralizes poison's toxic effects in the body, doing good will always help to conquer evil's effects in you.

The healthier you become, the more patient and merciful you will be toward broken and even destructive people. (See Jesus' instructions on how to love these kinds of people in Luke 6:27-36.) The apostle Paul says,

> We bless those who curse us. We are patient with those who abuse us. We appeal gently when evil things are said about us. Yet we are treated like the world's garbage, like everybody's trash—right up to the present moment (1 Corinthians 4:12-13).

Paul learned how to keep people from pushing his emotional buttons and how to respond with goodness when they were destructive toward him. Loving his enemies didn't mean Paul had a close personal relationship with them, nor did he ever minimize their destructiveness. But he didn't attack them or treat them as he was treated. He genuinely desired what was best for them, which was their repentance. Both Jesus and Paul taught these difficult lessons, and it is for our absolute good that we learn them. Otherwise, evil will quickly overtake us and we will become like the very thing we hate. The psalmist cried out, "Guide my steps by your word, so I will not be overcome by evil" (Psalm 119:133).

Beyond Victim to Victor

Our personal story is not over. We are still in progress…just like my basement. It has come a long way since I started writing this book. The carpet's laid, the desks are back in place, and the filing cabinets are where they should be, but there are still many things that need to be organized, thrown out, and put away. Little by little I will accomplish these remaining tasks, but my office is much better today than it was just months ago.

I hope that you're beginning to make some changes in the way you're handling the destructive relationships you're in. Maybe everything's not quite the way you want it and you still have things to change, but you're moving forward. A crucial part of your healing will occur when you no longer see yourself as a victim but begin learning how you can become the victor.

In the history of the Jews, God often promised Israel she would defeat her opponents, but he still required her participation. God has laid out a battle plan for you to overcome evil; are you willing to do battle and fight? Are you willing to put on your armor and let go of your own destructive ways? Are you willing to abandon thoughts and feelings that are contrary to God's best for your healing and growth? Or, like the ten spies who doubted God's promises, are you too afraid of the giants in your landscape to believe that God will help you and give you the victory?

Throughout the biblical narrative, we read of individuals who were healed and changed by God's loving grace. Many of them begin their stories by saying something like, "Once I was lost, but now I'm found." Or, "Once I was blind, but now I can see."

Take a moment and look back over your life. See where you were and how far you've come. What strengths have you gained? What hindrances have you let go of? In what areas do you need more practice, so that you can stand stronger in the future? Name some specific ways that you are overcoming evil with good, not only for your own benefit, but also for the future of your children, as well as for the glory of God.

Your story is only a part of a much bigger drama. God is using *you* to show people what he is like. Are you beginning to resemble him? Someone once said that we are what we are not because of what happens to us, but because of what we do with what happens to us. My friend, choose to do good with what's happened to you, and you will be better for it.

Recently the same friend who wrote the poem at the end of chapter 11 shared with me another short poem, which summarized where she was in her journey toward healing and wholeness. She gave me permission to share it as well with you:

> *The legacy I'd like to leave behind*
> *Is that I've helped one life at a time*
> *Beginning with mine.*

—DONNA UPSON, 2006

It is my prayer that you too will practice what you've learned. Allow God to love you, strengthen you, and heal you, so that your life might be and become all it was meant to be.

Resources for Further Help

Today it is not difficult to find information and support for every topic imaginable. What can be confusing is having to sort through the maze of choices. Below are some resources that I have found useful in my work with those caught in destructive relationships. Some are Christian, while others are secular but still very helpful.

Don't get overwhelmed into inaction because of the wealth of information available to you. Knowledge can be extremely helpful in determining a wise course of action, learning that your feelings are normal considering your situation, and discovering what works and what doesn't. Above all, your most valuable resource will be your Bible. Read it often. It will give you comfort, guidance, and wisdom. It is a love letter from God to help you live well.

Recommended Reading List

Bancroft, Lundy. *Why Does He Do That? Inside the Minds of Angry and Controlling Men.* Berkley Publishing Group, 2002. This is a terrific resource to help pastors and counselors understand the minds of abusive, controlling men and what needs to change in order for reconciliation to be possible.

Cloud, Henry, and John Townsend. *Boundaries in Marriage.* Zondervan, 2002. Written by Christian psychologists who explain what boundaries are and why they are important in any healthy marriage. Their other book, *Boundaries,* (Zondervan, 2002), also gives important guidance to those who feel guilty when they try to say no to people.

Evans, Patricia. *The Verbally Abusive Relationship: How to Recognize It and How to Respond.* Adams Media Corporation, 1996. This secular but very helpful book is written to help those who find themselves scratching their heads and wondering why they can't seem to communicate effectively with their partners. Evans describes many types of verbal abuse and gives readers practical strategies on how to handle the controlling and verbally abusive person. I don't find her section on the causes of abusive behavior as helpful as Bancroft's book.

McDill, S.R. and Linda McDill. *Dangerous Marriage: Breaking the Cycle of Domestic Violence.* Spire Press, 1999. This is a small but helpful book for those in abusive marriages. Although primarily secularly trained, these authors provide good insight and advice directed specifically to Christians trapped in violent marriages.

Seamands, David E. *Healing for Damaged Emotions.* Chariot Victor, 1981. Readable and helpful Christian resource for those who have been emotionally wounded by others. Seamands helps readers identify the lies they've believed and how to break these lies' emotional hold.

Silvious, Jan. *Fool-Proofing Your Life: An Honorable Way to Deal with the Impossible People in Your Life.* WaterBrook, 1998. Using the book of Proverbs, Silvious helps people learn how to recognize a fool and adopt strategies for being in relationship with one.

Vernick, Leslie. *How to Act Right When Your Spouse Acts Wrong.* WaterBrook, 2001. Whether in big ways or small ways, when our spouses do things we don't like, we often have a hard time responding to the behavior in a God-honoring way. This book helps the offended partner learn to see what God's purpose is through the difficult seasons of marriage and why it is good for them to learn these lessons.

Welch, Edward T. *When People Are Big and God Is Small: Overcoming Peer Pressure, Codependency and the Fear of Man.* P & R Publishing, 1997. This is an excellent Christian resource for those who continue to repeat unhealthy relationship patterns because they are too afraid of rejection or disapproval to speak up or stand up.

Phone Numbers for Information and Help

In an emergency, or if you are in danger dial 9-1-1.

National Domestic Violence Hotline
800-799-SAFE (7233)
800-787-3224 (TDD)

Staffed 24 hours a day by trained counselors who provide crisis counseling, safety planning, and assistance in finding local resources, shelters, and counseling. This resource is not limited to those experiencing physical violence but provides help for any type of destructive relationship.

Lighthouse Network
877-562-2565

This is a free hotline linking those struggling in abusive relationships (victim or perpetrator) and in need of treatment options for behavioral, emotional, stress, or substance abuse issues to Christian care/resources (or best secular if Christian not desired or available)—either outpatient counseling, inpatient, detox, or rehab.

Family Renewal Shelter
24-hour crisis line: 253-475-9010
National 24-hour crisis line: 888-550-3915

This Christian resource provides crisis help and safety planning for victims of abusive relationships. They also have limited shelter services for women and their children who are in high-risk situations.

Web Sites

Awake, Inc.
www.awakeonline.org

Offers various resources and biblical helps for recognizing and stopping destructive relationship patterns. See their abuse page, where you can download information on developing a safety plan if you are in a dangerous relationship.

The Black Church and Domestic Violence Institute
www.bcdvi.org

This organization works to develop partnerships and collaborations to provide educational, spiritual, and technical support as well as advocacy and leadership development; to enhance the capacity of the church to empower and protect the victims of domestic violence; to hold abusers accountable; to promote healing and wholeness in African–American communities.

Bridging the Gap
www.bridgingthegap.freeservers.com

Provides information, training support groups, and workshops for religious leaders and human-service professionals in preventing and addressing the issues of abuse, addiction, and domestic violence.

Christians in Recovery
www.christians-in-recovery.com

This site is a comprehensive resource for people recovering from abuse, family dysfunction, relationship problems, and pornography. It contains valuable information and resources to help you help yourself. A Members Only section offers private chat rooms, daily scheduled recovery meetings, e-mail groups, message boards, twelve-step Bible studies, and more.

FaithTrust Institute
www.faithtrustinstitute.org

FaithTrust Institute, formerly the Center for Prevention of Sexual and Domestic Violence, offers a wide range of services and resources, including training, consultation, and educational materials, to provide communities and advocates with the tools and knowledge they need to address the religious and cultural issues related to abuse. They are a multifaith organization.

Family Renewal Shelter
www.domesticviolencehelp.org

Family Renewal Shelter is a Christian humanitarian organization dedicated to bring healing, hope, and new life to victims of domestic violence. They have a crisis line as well as provide help to friends and families on what to say to both victims and abusers alike. They also provide limited shelter for those seeking refuge. Their sheltering services are limited to extremely high-risk victims of physical violence.

FOCUS Ministries
www.focusministries1.org

Focus Ministries is a Christian not-for-profit organization devoted to offering hope, encouragement, education, and assistance to women who are struggling in difficult circumstances, especially dysfunctional marriages, spousal abuse, separation, or divorce. Their locations are in the Chicago, Illinois, area and Madisonville, Kentucky.

Lighthouse Network
www.lighthousenetwork.org

Christian ministry with the mission to help people develop better daily decision-making and relationship skills. Produces a bimonthly newsletter and much educational information to help people relate to God, others, and self in more healthy ways to achieve their God-given potential.

National Association for Christian Recovery (NACR)
www.christianrecovery.com

This site seeks to equip the church with Christ-centered and outreach-oriented recovery strategies. NACR helps Christians integrate recovery with faith and provides support for those involved in the growing recovery network. The organization publishes *Steps,* a quarterly magazine containing information on Christian support groups, workshops, and conferences.

National Latino Alliance for the Elimination of Domestic Violence
www.dvalianza.org

Provides resources for victims of abuse, advocates political action, and educates members of the local community.

PASCH
www.peaceandsafety.com

This organization sponsors conferences and specific helps to promote peace and safety in Christian homes. It has valuable information on developing a safety plan and offers free telephone consultation.

Shattered Men
www.shatteredmen.com

This Christian interactive Yahoo! club deals with destructive and abusive relationships of all kinds, but specifically offers men opportunities to find support when they are the victims of these kinds of relationships.

Women's Faith Force Ministry
www.womensfaithforceministry.org

This organization provides information for teaching, training, and educating people on the issues related to partner abuse.

Categories of Abuse

⁓

A buse can be categorized as physical, verbal and emotional, or sexual.

Physical abuse is characterized by hitting, slapping, spitting at, punching, kicking, yanking (such as by the hair or limbs), throwing, banging, biting, restraining, or any act of physical coercion or violence directed at another person. Abusers attempt to control and intimidate others through violence, and also by creating an atmosphere or environment of anticipated violence. They might raise a fist, bang on a wall, or wave a gun in someone's face.

These kinds of behaviors are abusive even if they do not result in visible injury to the victim. Abusive actions demonstrate profound disrespect for the well-being of the other person. If someone did these things to a stranger or in public, the conduct would unquestionably be considered abusive and the perpetrator might even be arrested.

Wherever there is physical abuse, there is always verbal and emotional abuse. Often sexual abuse is also part of the overall abusive pattern.

Verbal and emotional abuse occurs when words and gestures are the weapons used to hurt, destroy, or control and dominate another person. We often underestimate the power of words to harm others and can be unsympathetic to those trapped in verbally abusive relationships. We say things like "Don't let it bother you," or "Just let it roll off your back." We all remember the nursery rhyme, "Sticks and stones will break your bones, but words will never hurt me." But God knows how words affect our emotional, spiritual, and physical health. For example, Proverbs says, "Reckless words pierce like a sword" (12:18 NIV), and, "Wise words bring many benefits" (12:14). "Gentle words are a tree of life; a deceitful tongue crushes the spirit" (Proverbs 15:4). "Kind words are like honey—sweet to the soul and healthy for the body" (Proverbs 16:24).

Most often we think of name-calling, cursing, profanity, and mocking when we think of verbal abuse. However, verbal abuse can also include constant criticism and blaming; discounting or devaluing the feelings, thoughts, and opinions of another; as well as manipulating words to deceive, mislead, or confuse someone.

Emotional abuse can also be characterized by degrading someone, embarrassing them publicly, or humiliating them in front of family, friends, or work associates. Nonphysical abuse employs more than words to hurt another. Emotional abusers systematically undermine their victim in order to gain control. Abusers weaken others in order to strengthen themselves. They know what matters most to their target (for example, her children, his work, her appearance, her family, his pet, her friends), and they seek to destroy it.

Sexual abuse occurs whenever one person forces an unwilling party into having sexual relations or performing sexual acts, even within a marriage. Recently while teaching a class on domestic violence at a seminary, a student challenged my definition.

The seminary student argued that 1 Corinthians 7 was biblical proof that forcing a wife to have sex with her husband could not be considered abusive because it was biblically wrong for a wife to refuse her husband. From his perspective, it was a man's God-given right to force his wife if she denied him.

It is true that the apostle Paul cautions husbands and wives not to deprive each other of sexual relations except under special circumstances. However, Paul also wrote that husbands are to love their wives as Christ loved the church (Ephesians 5:25). Paul describes what that kind of love looks like; it is a giving and cherishing love, not a coercing or disrespectful love (Ephesians 5; 1 Corinthians 13).

If a wife sexually refuses her husband, whatever her reason may be, a loving husband would never respond to his legitimate disappointment by forcing his wife to have sex against her will. At most he might try to gently change her mind, but likely he will accept her decision and try again another time. If his wife regularly denies him, ideally he would pray for her as well as ask her what the problem is, encourage her to work on the problem herself, or go for help together. Forcing his wife to have sex against her will reduces her to an object for him to use as he sees fit regardless of her feelings. That is not only degrading and disrespectful to his wife, it is abusive.

Other forms of sexual abuse include touching others sexually without their permission, pressuring them to view or participate in pornography, talking to them in sexually derogatory or humiliating ways, taking sexually explicit pictures without their permission, or making uninvited suggestive comments.

All abuse is emotionally destructive and negates the personhood of the victim. A healthy relationship is impossible in the presence of any kind of ongoing or unrepentant abuse.

A Special Word to People Helpers

Whether you are a friend, relative, clergy member, or professional counselor, you may find yourself unsure or unprepared when you hear the stories of people caught in destructive relationships. In this short appendix I cannot equip you with everything you need to know to help someone, but I want to give you some important information that will make you more effective and compassionate.

1. Be patient. What seems like a clear solution to us isn't so clear to the person stuck in a destructive relationship pattern. Sometimes you may be tempted to give up or pull away when your efforts to help someone seem ineffective. Please don't. It often takes a long time for someone to get ready to make a significant change in an important relationship, even if that relationship is quite painful.

Consider that God has put this person in your life right now for a reason. You have an opportunity to incarnate Christ and model a healthy relationship as you lovingly walk beside him or her during this difficult time. Following are some specific things to keep in mind during what might be a long process.

2. Listen carefully. God's Word tells us that answering someone before fully listening is foolish (Proverbs 18:13). One of the best gifts you can give someone who is hurting is your undivided attention and attentive ear. You may not know what to say, or you may think you know exactly what to say. In either case, hold off. The best way to communicate that you have heard someone is to gently repeat or paraphrase back what you think you heard them say.

When people know you have heard them fully, they will be more ready to hear what you might have to say.

3. Don't dismiss the person's feelings or situation. What may feel tolerable to one person may feel unbearable to another. Don't minimize or trivialize others' pain because you can't understand why they feel as they do. When I was pregnant, I remember hearing women tell of their experiences with natural childbirth that made it seem not too bad. I felt like a total failure when, after ten hours of labor, I gave up and requested (more like demanded) drugs. People are unique, and each of us has different thresholds for emotional pain as well as tolerance for stress.

4. If the person discloses that a partner exhibits abusive or controlling attitudes or actions, be careful. Many professional counselors as well as pastors never receive any specialized training in recognizing abusive relationships nor know how to assess danger. That doesn't mean you can't care, listen, and help, but be wary of telling someone what he or she should or should not do, especially with respect to leaving an abusive partner or reconciling with one if already separated. The consequences are too grave to the person and any children involved if you are wrong.

There are three common mistakes people make when working with a person caught an abusive relationship. First, we may blame the victim. Abused people are not sinless, and so it's tempting to look for things they have done that provoked the abusive incidents.

We might say to a woman, "If only you had been more submissive or less argumentative, then your husband wouldn't have treated you this way." And we might be right—this time.

There are always at least two sides to every story, but abusive behavior is always a sin and never an appropriate response, even if provoked. As people helpers it is imperative never to justify or excuse sinful behavior by blaming the victim. People provoke us all the time, but that never justifies or excuses our sinful response. Moses was held accountable for his temper outbursts even though the Israelites had provoked him greatly (Numbers 20:1-12).

The second error people helpers make when working with abusive/controlling marriage partners is to do marriage counseling. All research on domestic violence indicates that marital counseling is contraindicated. The victim will not be free to be honest and the abuser will continue to intimidate and control, even in the counseling. Without specialized training in abusive relationship patterns, it is unwise to tackle these issues in a counseling relationship.

The third error we make is that we try to become a benevolent rescuer. We give advice to the victims, tell them what to do, think for them, and make decisions for them all out of compassion and fear for their well-being. On the surface this looks like the right thing to do for people who feel helpless and overwhelmed, but in the long run you are not helping them to mature and think for themselves. You are just substituting one controlling relationship for another. Their dependence is what made them vulnerable to being controlled in the first place. Taking over when they should be learning to think for themselves will not help them to grow.

5. Help the person carefully weigh his or her options and the potential consequences of these choices. One of the best things you can do is to become a sounding board that helps someone to think through pros and cons. Many times no alternative looks easy. Pain and confusion prevent many people from thinking clearly or being mindful of all their options. Advise in a calm, nonjudgmental manner. Don't push the solutions you would choose on the person. You may be able to point out things that hinder good choices, and then help the person work through those obstacles in order to grow. You can also help him or her practice the speak-up dialogues and role play in preparation for wise and calm confrontations with a relationship partner.

6. *Be honest about your limitations.* Don't promise to do what you can't fulfill in the long run. Most of us are more than willing to answer distress calls in the middle of the night once in a while, but a regular pattern will grow tiresome sooner or later. No one can be all present, all knowing, and all loving at all times. It is important to recognize your limitations and continue to point the person to depend on God for strength and wisdom. We can be used by God, but we are not God.

7. *Be prayerful.* After all is said and done, you may feel rather impotent to help someone struggling in a destructive relationship. He or she may be unwilling to take action to evade danger or change the destructive patterns. Remember, you are *not* helpless. Prayer is a potent reminder that God is in charge and loves both individuals caught in their destructive dance. Take them before God daily, asking him to intervene in ways that you cannot imagine.

At the close of each of my counseling sessions, I usually ask my clients if I can pray for them. Prayer reminds us that there is a greater source of help than I can provide. Pray with people every chance you get. I have rarely encountered someone who didn't deeply appreciate a personal prayer.

8. *Be practical.* Sometimes we forget that at times the most helpful thing we can do is to provide tangible help. The person may need

medical attention, professional counseling, phone numbers for shelters, legal help, or information about community resources.

Become an expert on what's available in your locale, and provide a list of competent referral sources that the person can use to build a support system. You can't build or be the whole support system, but you can provide a start.

Notes

Chapter 1—What Is an Emotionally Destructive Relationship?

1. The psychological term for this behavior is *gaslighting*, which comes from the 1944 film *Gaslight*, in which a husband makes his wife think she is going crazy.

Chapter 2—The Consequences of an Emotionally Destructive Relationship

1. Daniel Goleman, *Social Intelligence: The New Science of Human Relationships* (New York: Bantam Books, 2006), 4.

2. See my book *How to Act Right When Your Spouse Acts Wrong* (Colorado Springs, CO: WaterBrook Press, 2003) for additional help in learning how to respond instead of react, and how to overcome evil with good during seasons of marital distress.

3. Goleman, 13.

4. Goleman, 5.

5. Sari N. Harrar, "Tongue-lashing Leaves Scars," *Prevention,* July 2006, 38.

6. Jeanie Lerche Davis, "The Heart Speaks (Are You Listening?)," interview with Mimi Guarneri, *WebMD,* http://aolsvc.health.webmd.aol.com/content/Article/119/113218.htm (accessed March 12, 2006).

7. Goleman, 152.

8. Goleman, 161.

Chapter 3—What Makes Relationships Difficult and Destructive?

1. Wayne Grudem, *Systematic Theology* (Grand Rapids, MI: Zondervan, 1994), 498.

2. In my book *How to Find Selfless Joy in a Me-First World* (Colorado Springs, CO: WaterBrook Press, 2003), I explore the themes of self-esteem, self-love, and

humility, and how problems in these areas impact and affect our relationship with God, our relationship with others, and our relationship with ourselves.

3. At times Jesus uses the terms *sinfulness* and *sickness* together in his teaching. For example, he says, "Healthy people don't need a doctor—sick people do. I have come to call sinners, not those who think they are already good enough" (Mark 2:17). Sickness and sinfulness are both consequences of the fall and our subsequent brokenness.

4. Thomas Dubay, *The Evidential Power of Beauty: Science and Theology Meet* (San Francisco: Ignatius Press, 1999), 17.

5. Walter A. Elwell, *Evangelical Dictionary of Theology* (Grand Rapids, MI: Baker Book House, 2001), 967.

Chapter 4—Destructive Themes of the Heart: Pride, Anger, and Envy

1. *NIV Study Bible,* Tenth Anniversary ed. (Grand Rapids, MI: Zondervan, 1995), 783.

2. Solomon Schimmel, *The Seven Deadly Sins: Jewish, Christian, and Classical Reflections on Human Psychology* (New York: Oxford University Press, 1997), 43.

3. Schimmel, 50.

4. Lundy Bancroft, *Why Does He Do That? Inside the Minds of Angry and Controlling Men* (New York: Berkley Publishing Group, 2002), 39.

5. Schimmel, 83.

6. Mark Rutland, *Behind the Glittering Mask* (Ann Arbor, MI: Servant Publications, 1996), 62.

Chapter 5—Destructive Themes of the Heart: Selfishness, Laziness, Evil, and Fear

1. Henry Fairlie, *The Seven Deadly Sins Today* (Notre Dame, IN: University of Notre Dame Press, 1979), 40-41.

2. Fairlie, 114.

3. Mark Rutland, *Behind the Glittering Mask* (Ann Arbor, MI: Servant Publications, 1996), 110.

4. M. Scott Peck, *The Road Less Traveled,* (New York: Simon & Schuster, 1978), 271.

5. Spiros Zodhiates, ed., *The Complete Word Study New Testament* (Chattanooga, TN: AMG Publishers, 1991), 924.

6. Dan Allender, *Bold Love* (Colorado Springs, CO: NavPress Publishing Group, 1992), 238.

7. David Benner, *The Gift of Being Yourself: The Sacred Call to Self-Discovery* (Downers Grove, IL: InterVarsity Press, 2004), 81.

Chapter 6—The Truth About Change: You Can Stop Living This Way

1. Despite her best effort, the author was unable to locate the writer of this e-mail. If information comes to light, the author will be pleased to give proper acknowledgment in future editions of this book.

2. David Seamands, *Healing of Memories* (Colorado Springs, CO: Chariot Victor, 1985), 165.

3. Janet Kornblum, "One-Quarter of Americans Have No One to Confide In," USAToday.com, June 23, 2006, accessed at http://articles.news.aol.com/news/article.adp?id=20060623073209990027&_ccc=6&cid=8. Based on a study from the General Social Survey by the National Opinion Research Center at the University of Chicago.

4. In "Husbands and Wives as Analogues of Christ and the Church," George W. Knight III says, "The New Testament never commands husbands to subordinate their wives, i.e., to force them to submit. The voice of the verb is not active but middle/passive, with the meaning either of subjecting oneself (middle) or of allowing oneself to be in subjection (passive), with the middle voice most likely here." Article found in John Piper and Wayne Grudem, eds., *Recovering Biblical Manhood and Womanhood: A Response to Evangelical Feminism* (Wheaton, IL: Crossway Books, 1991), 169.

Chapter 7—The Truth About Choices: They Have Not Been Taken from You

1. Viktor Frankl, *Man's Search For Meaning: An Introduction to Logotherapy* (New York: Simon & Schuster, 1984), 75.

Chapter 8—The Truth About Speaking Up: Your Voice Deserves to Be Heard

1. For more information on developing a safety plan in an abusive relationship, read Ann Jones and Susan Schechter's book *When Love Goes Wrong: What to Do When You Can't Do Anything Right: Strategies for Women with Controlling Partners* (New York: HarperPerennial, 1992). This is an extremely helpful, practical book for anyone struggling with a controlling partner. It gives very specific steps in

developing a safety plan, how to protect your children, finding a safe place to stay if you plan to leave, and dealing with the police and legal system.

You can also call 1-800-799-SAFE (7233) to talk to a trained abuse counselor. Also see "Resources for Further Help" in the back of this book.

Chapter 9—The Truth About Standing Up: You Can Become a Champion of Peace

1. W. A. Elwell and P. W. Comfort, *Tyndale Bible Dictionary* (Wheaton, IL: Tyndale House Publishers, 2001), 1004.

2. C.S. Lewis, *The Problem of Pain* (New York: Dodd Mead, 1935), 19.

Chapter 10—God Sees You and Wants to Heal You

1. J. Swanson, *Dictionary of Biblical Languages with Semantic Domains: Greek New Testament,* electronic ed. (Oak Harbor, WA: Logos Research Systems, Inc., 1997), GGK3701.

2. Richard Rohr, *Everything Belongs: The Gift of Contemplative Prayer* (New York: Crossroads Publishing Company, 2003), 131.

3. Rohr, 29.

4. Rohr, 69.

5. B. Patterson and D.L. Goetz, *Deepening Your Conversation with God* (Minneapolis, MN: Bethany House Publishers, 1999), 59.

Chapter 11—If You Let Go, You Will Grow

1. This exercise, as well as the research mentioned in this chapter, is from Christopher Peterson, *A Primer in Positive Psychology* (New York: Oxford University Press, 2006).

2. In my book *How to Act Right When Your Spouse Acts Wrong,* I cover more extensively this concept of extending forgiveness even when the relationship is not or cannot be reconciled because of unrepentant sin (Colorado Springs, CO: WaterBrook Press, 2001).

3. Daniel Goleman, *Social Intelligence* (New York: Bantam Books, 2006), 44-45.

4. In a study cited in *A Primer in Positive Psychology* (34-35), college students were asked which satisfied them more—having a good time or helping others. To answer that question, they were told to pursue one pleasurable activity (of their own choice) and one philanthropic activity (of their own choice), then write a

brief paper about their reactions to each. Overwhelmingly, the students discovered that fun was pleasurable for the moment, but deeper satisfaction came when they helped others or did something good for someone else.

5. M. Scott Peck, *The Road Less Traveled* (New York: Simon & Schuster, 1978), 58.

6. J. Strong, *The Exhaustive Concordance of the Bible,* electronic ed., (Ontario: Woodside Bible Fellowship, 1996), G4991.

Chapter 12—When You're Properly Nourished, You Will Thrive

1. For more information on learning how to handle conflict, see my book *Getting Over the Blues: A Woman's Guide to Handling Depression* (Eugene, OR: Harvest House Publishers, 2005), chapter 9.

About the Author

Leslie Vernick is a licensed clinical social worker with a private counseling practice near Allentown, Pennsylvania. She is the author of *How to Live Right When Your Life Goes Wrong, How to Act Right When Your Spouse Acts Wrong, How to Find Selfless Joy in a Me-First World,* and *Getting Over the Blues.* She has also contributed to the *Soul Care Bible, Competent Christian Counseling,* and numerous other books. She is an active member of the American Association of Christian Counselors and teaches in two of their video series: *Marriage Works* and *Extraordinary Women.*

Leslie and her husband, Howard, have been married for more than 30 years and are the proud parents of two grown children, Ryan and Amanda.

Leslie is a popular speaker at conferences, women's retreats, and couples' retreats. She loves to encourage and motivate people to deepen their relationship with God and others. For more information on Leslie's work and ministry, visit her Web site at www.leslievernick.com.

Harvest House Books to Help You Grow Spiritually and Emotionally

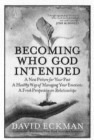

BECOMING WHO GOD INTENDED
A New Picture for Your Past • A Healthy Way of Managing Your Emotions • A Fresh Perspective on Relationships

David Eckman

Whether you realize it or not, your imagination is filled with *pictures* of reality. The Bible indicates these pictures reveal your true "heart beliefs"—the beliefs that actually shape your everyday feelings and reactions to family and friends, to your life circumstances, and to God.

David Eckman compassionately shows you how to allow God's Spirit to build new, *biblical* pictures in your heart and imagination. As you do this, you will be able to break free of negative emotions...and finally experience the life God has always intended for you.

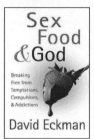

SEX, FOOD, AND GOD
Breaking Free from Temptations, Compulsions, and Addictions

David Eckman

The good things created by God, like food and sex, can be misused to run away from emotional/relational pain. When this happens, the damage and loneliness can be worse than the worst nightmare.

Using groundbreaking research and offering compassionate understanding rooted deeply in the Bible, David Eckman shares

- how and why unhealthy appetites grip and trap people in a fantasy world
- how shame and guilt disappear when we realize how much God delights in us
- how four great experiences of the spiritual life break the addiction cycle

FROM FAKING IT TO FINDING GRACE
Discovering God Again When Your Faith Runs Dry

Connie Cavanaugh

Spiritual dryness and disillusionment—nobody ever talks about them. But the truth is, almost every believer experiences periods of feeling disconnected from God.

Writer and speaker Connie Cavanaugh speaks out of her own ten-year struggle. You can trust her to mentor you toward a deeper and more mature friendship with God. "You're not alone in this," she says, "so hold on to hope—He's calling you back."

HARVEST HOUSE
PUBLISHERS

Harvest House Books to Help You
Grow Spiritually and Emotionally

YOUR SCARS ARE BEAUTIFUL TO GOD
Finding Peace and Purpose in the Hurts of Your Past

Sharon Jaynes

Physical scars represent a story, a moment in your life, and they show others there is a history and a healing. Your internal scars—invisible marks from heartbreak, mistakes, and losses—also represent stories of healing and restoration. Author Sharon Jaynes's gentle insight will help you give your wounds to the One who sees your beauty and who can turn pain into purpose and heartache into hope as you...

- recognize Jesus through your scars
- remove the mask and be real
- release the power of healed wounds

THE CONFIDENT WOMAN
Knowing Who You Are in Christ

Anabel Gillham

Do you struggle to be the "perfect Christian" for God, your family, your employer, your friends? You're not alone. But God doesn't call you to be "perfect." He calls you to be *confident*—because of His love, His acceptance, and the life of His Son, Jesus, inside you. Anabel Gillham shares with you God's plan for freedom, rest, and peace, showing you from Scripture what a truly confident woman looks like.

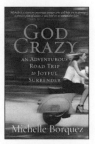

GOD CRAZY
An Adventurous Road Trip to Joyful Surrender

Michelle Borquez

"God crazy" is the remarkable heart change that happens when you leap into God's purpose and never look back. After maintaining the appearance of an ideal marriage and life, Michelle Borquez's façade finally shattered. In that brokenness she discovered—as you can—a renewed, passionate love for Christ and a hunger for deeper faith. She leads you to that point of transformation where faith is not just a belief but your inspiration to soar as you...

- give your life over to God's lead
- embrace *la vida loca* ideas for your faith journey
- discover and pursue the desires of your heart

HARVEST HOUSE
PUBLISHERS

To learn more about any Harvest House Book
or to read sample chapters, log on to our website:

www.harvesthousepublishers.com

HARVEST HOUSE PUBLISHERS

EUGENE, OREGON